Getting Things Done Where All Politics Is Local

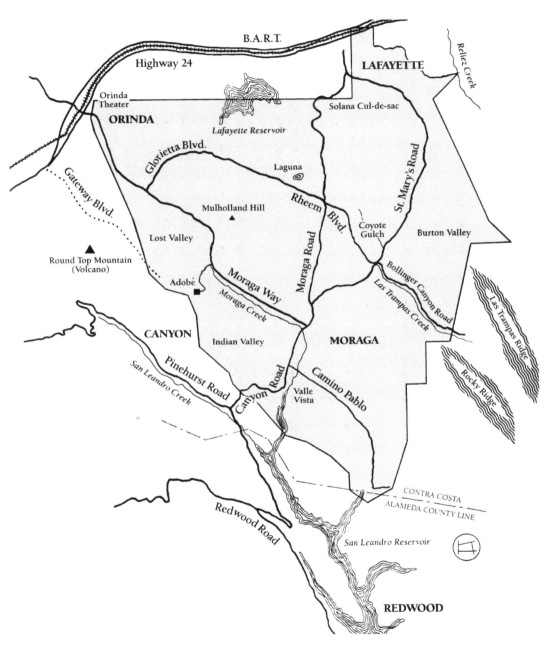

The Moraga Rancho today.
(from Kimball)

Getting Things Done Where All Politics Is Local

MICHAEL FRENCH METCALF

White River Press
Amherst, Massachusetts

First published by White River Press LLC,
Amherst, Massachusetts • whiteriverpress.com

ISBN: 979-8-88545-020-1

Book cover and interior designed by Lufkin Graphic Designs
Norwich, Vermont • www.LufkinGraphics.com

Cover photos and credits:
    Front: Children Flying a Kite; Moraga Commons entrance (Sharon Bartlett Metcalf)
              Wedding at Hacienda de las Flores (Town of Moraga)
    Back: Michael Metcalf (Sharon Bartlett Metcalf)

Library of Congress Cataloging-in-Publication Data

Names: Metcalf, Michael French, 1941- author.
Title: Getting things done where all politics is local / Michael French
  Metcalf.
Description: Amherst, Massachusetts : White River Press, [2024]
Identifiers: LCCN 2024020866 | ISBN 9798885450201 (trade paperback)
Subjects: LCSH: Metcalf, Michael French, 1941- |
  Mayors--California--Moraga--Biography. | Moraga (Calif.)--Politics and
  government--21st century. | Moraga (Calif.)--History--21st century. |
  Moraga (Calif.)--Biography.
Classification: LCC F869.M756 M48 2024 | DDC 979.4/63092
  [B]--dc23/eng/20240503
LC record available at https://lccn.loc.gov/2024020866

Dedication

This story is dedicated to . . .

Mike Segrest, Moraga Town Manager (2009-2010), for his inspiration
and imaginative approaches to changes in Moraga; and to
Jill Keimach, Moraga Town Manager (2010-16), for her competence in delivering
critical projects and doing so with wonderful charm and sensitivity.

Moraga was blessed with the services of these two exceptional people.

Contents

Foreword

I RECALL FIRST MEETING MIKE METCALF in 1999, a few months after his appointment to the Moraga Planning Commission. We met at a dinner party celebrating Jay Tashiro, Moraga's longtime planning director, and his hiring as the new city manager of another Bay Area city, the year after I concluded a seven-year stint on the commission.

Usually planning commissioners volunteer for the job because they want to serve and give back to their local community. Some may just be trying to "polish their resumes." But that is not the case here. In Mike, the commitment to public service was there, and more. From the outset, Mike struck me as a serious person. He was very focused and intent on "getting things done." So was I.

That strong impression of Mike stuck with me in the years that followed—especially after Mike was elected to the Moraga Town Council in 2004. Two years later I joined him, and we served as colleagues on the council for the next ten years (2006-2016).

So when Mike asked me to write the foreword to his latest book, *Getting Things Done Where All Politics Is Local*, I was happy to oblige.

Taking Tip O'Neill's famous adage as a springboard, *Getting Things Done* examines the key intersection between local politics and public policy. Mike writes persuasively on why elected leaders need to understand, inform and educate their constituents, and endeavor in that process to shape local politics and public opinion, in order to successfully achieve important public policy goals.

Mike and I occupy different parts of the spectrum of local politics. We did not agree on everything—not by any means. But we shared some common values: We believed that the council wasn't and shouldn't just be an ineffectual "debating society." And we believed that some positive changes in Moraga were long overdue. Working together and with support from our council colleagues, we succeeded in accomplishing some beneficial things in the broader public interest. Mike writes cogently about several of these accomplishments in this book . . . and about other initiatives that ultimately weren't successful, and the reasons why (at least in his opinion).

Mike insists his book is not meant to be a work of history. Since it is a personal and admittedly subjective account, this is to some extent true. But that isn't the whole story. While Mike might not have intended it, in some interesting and important respects *Getting Things Done Where All Politics Is Local* picks up where *Moraga's Pride* (2d. ed 2002), the seminal work on the history of the Moraga Rancho, leaves off.

I believe readers of this book—including folks who cherish our local history—will appreciate Mike's story, political memoir, and insights into Moraga's history.

David W. Trotter
Moraga, California
November 2024

Preface

ALL POLITICS IS LOCAL. That aphorism was used in the 1980s by Tip O'Neill, a former Speaker of the U.S. House of Representatives, who remains closely associated with the phrase. It's said he didn't originate it, but that doesn't matter. What the august Speaker from the Commonwealth of Massachusetts said then, has resonated with me since. His words were on my mind when I became involved in local politics in my hometown of Moraga, California, on the cusp of the new millennium. Indeed, his words became something of a beacon for me as I ventured into the foray of the local politics that were a constant swirl in my small town. The town was engulfed in myriad disputes with some of its neighboring cities and there were quarrels amongst various institutions in the town. Even some of the citizens seemed at war with one another. Why would I become involved in what seemed a bit like civic combat? As I have looked back on my experiences, the answer to that question remains something of a mystery. Yet such retrospection has been helpful and, indeed, satisfying. For I believe I now understand more clearly what the sage old Bostonian might have meant. He clearly had something in mind that was grander in scale than a little suburban town like Moraga. But that didn't matter to me. I could understand how some principles of local politics applied in my hometown.

This book is a short story of my political adventures. I've written it to help clarify in my own mind why I did what I did, what motivated me, what I thought I might accomplish, and whether, at the end of the day, I could honestly say I'd been useful. With the benefit of hindsight, it's time to commit some thoughts to paper. Someone other than me might enjoy reading it— for me, just telling my story is enough. But sharing it with others makes it better.

As the twentieth century was ending, so was my professional career in engineering project management. I was about to enter retirement, and I was fearing I might not have anything very worthwhile to do. Useful occupation is critical to me, otherwise I would go insane. Perhaps my family would, too. So I volunteered for the Town of Moraga, like many others have done in the past and many more will do in the future. One thing led to another, and my involvement became much deeper than I could have imagined. What happened over an eighteen-year period was both important and trivial, interesting and dull, serious and hilarious, satisfying and frustrating. A little of everything; sometimes too much of some. A lot was accomplished, and some actual things were enjoyed by many. Yet there were some disappointments. But whatever the outcome of the matter at hand, my personal growth was fortunate, albeit sometimes humbling. On balance, the rewards outweighed the disappointments, so I can conclude it was worth the effort.

Reconstructing the years of my public service was a challenge. Refreshing my memories of specific events was straightforward, as I relied on robust internet sources, Town of Moraga records, and my personal files. But the greatest challenge was how to tell the story. After all, the story is all about people. It's the people surrounding events that made the difference between something getting accomplished or not. Some of these people were terrific individuals, and some were not. I have refrained from referring to individuals by name unless their contributions to the story reflect kindly on them. If they are identified, and perhaps quoted, in a public medium such as a newspaper, I've had no reservations repeating what's already been made public. Otherwise, specific people are incognito.

This is not meant to be a work of history. What is reported actually happened. Most things are a matter of record, some are not. Numerous things are reflections of my personal views on the subject at hand. As such, a lot of my own opinions have surfaced. Because this is a story of my personal experiences, in my view, I was at liberty to state how I felt—and feel—about things. One can quibble with what I say, but not about my feelings.

Why would anyone be interested in reading about an ordinary citizen who busied himself thinking he was making a difference? Cynical people may scoff at such a book. On the other hand, some might like to read it. Because the story is not just about me. It's about them. Many people volunteer just as I did. Many of them finish with the satisfaction of knowing they did their best to make things better. In their eyes, they were useful. Those who have not yet volunteered might like to read about the experiences of someone who already has. They might appreciate the opportunity to see how such public service can be satisfying and important for personal growth. It's in that spirit that I'm sharing this short story. To me, it's all part of being useful.

Michael French Metcalf
Moraga, California
November 2024

CHAPTER 1

Introduction

W E BEGIN WITH A BIT OF BACKGROUND INFORMATION about me, the one who thought he could make a difference. After touching on my professional career, the story moves into my "retirement" phase, when I had the opportunity to change gears entirely. This led to my appointment to an important and very formal commission in my hometown, which evolved in time to a lengthy period on the Moraga Town Council. And that was when my political awakenings occurred, and where I believe I was doing things that were useful—the subject of this book.

Professional Career

After college and earning a degree in civil engineering in 1964, I joined the US Navy, Civil Engineer Corps. It was the early years of the Vietnam War, and the draft board was eager to snatch up young engineering graduates and place them in the US Army Corps of Engineers. The Army Corps' major purpose in Vietnam was to clear land mines, or so it was said. I didn't believe that the Navy engineers did much of that. I was attracted to the Seabees, the construction branch of the Navy. As it happened, the Seabees did, in fact, clear land mines, but they also did all sorts of other useful construction aimed at military support and civilian aid. That motivated me.

I was especially fascinated by the Seabees' motto: Can Do! It was a creed every Seabee carries in his mind and heart, telling himself and anyone he encountered that he was there to get things done. That suited me just fine. My construction battalion built a lot of things, and we truly helped many of the Vietnamese who were not quarreling with Americans. I loved every minute of it—but not so much the business of land mines.

I did two year-long tours in Vietnam, then I volunteered to extend my active service as an officer in charge of construction in Thailand. For two more years I supervised contractors in building airfields, communications facilities, housing, roads, drainage works, and the like. That, too, was rewarding. Getting things done was what it was all about, and I loved it.

After resigning from active duty, I decided to study construction management, and in 1970, I entered Stanford University. That led to my involvement with an engineering and construction company in San Francisco, which introduced me to the field of marine engineering. While working there I dreamed up a novel construction method for a difficult marine construction problem, which my supervising professor believed I should advance as a doctoral level project. That I did, and after two more years I was a freshly minted PhD and was looking for a real job. Another engineering company in San Francisco liked my doctoral work and figured I could do good work for them, so they hired me. Seven years later, I had met most of the research and development objectives of the company who was paying my way. I was helping solve engineering challenges of building oil and gas facilities in the North Sea, off Western Australia, and offshore New Zealand. It seemed to me I was doing things that were worthwhile; it was an exciting time.

Chevron, the international oil and gas company (then called Standard Oil Company of California) hired me in 1980 to continue with my R&D work. That turned out not to be a good idea, since the internal politics at Chevron stymied any chance for me of achieving much. Fortunately, my supervisor realized I was spinning my wheels, and he steered me in the direction of engineering project management. It wasn't long before I formed and led small teams, and we developed several novel and interesting technical projects. We did some good work for the company.

But the real opportunity came when Chevron acquired Gulf Oil in 1985. One of Gulf's last oil discoveries was in the remote rainforest of the Southern Highlands of Papua New Guinea (PNG), the archipelago nation just north of Queensland, Australia. Chevron management, wanting to understand what Gulf had discovered, instructed me to go there and imagine how an oil and gas development project might be built there. I spent a week in the rainforest in the bush camp of an Australian surveying team. We flew over the vast rainforest extensively, trudged through the jungle for miles, and talked over terrain maps well into the evenings. The bush surveyors had lots of ideas; they were full of enthusiasm. There was no question it could be done . . . but it would be a challenge. So, I returned to California and delivered my opinion to a skeptical management. To my surprise, they instructed me to form a team and try to figure things out. I was summoned before Chevron's partners—all international oil companies in the hunt for new oil and gas fields—and I was expected to convince them that Chevron could work out a feasible oil field development. I did it.

For the next three years, my team did all the exploring, surveying, environmental studies, engineering, and planning for a major oil and gas field in the primitive rainforest in this barely known wilderness. The engineering challenges were enormous, and the environmental issues were daunting. In addition, a major oil production and export project would pose a classic confrontation between business interests' intent on resource extraction and environmentalists dedicated to protecting the largely undisturbed and pristine environment of PNG. However, the most challenging dimension of such a project would be the native peoples of the PNG Highlands. Theirs was a primitive culture—they survived by their wits and guile, often in savage ways. Indeed, a few of the people from the more remote highlands areas were known to be practicing cannibals, some proudly so. It would be understating things to say that one needed to mind one's manners around them. While they would work hard and could be extremely loyal, they could turn on you if they sensed you were doing them wrong. Payback was their way of settling a score. It was rough, and one's politics needed to be delicate. To deliver such a project would be an enormous undertaking; to do it without destroying the natural environment of the country would require exceptional care and extreme diligence; to do it all with the cooperation of the native population would be essential.

We did what was sufficient to convince Chevron management and their partners that the field could be developed responsibly. Engineering and environmental studies were completed; construction planning was undertaken; considerable progress was made toward convincing the PNG and local governments that Chevron would handle the development responsibly. Numerous excellent companies were hired to do the nitty-gritty, and things were taking shape. Moreover, the project made economic sense, so Chevron and its partners approved the Kutubu Oil Field development in 1988.[1]

The project team then commenced the detailed work. This was not something I much cared for; my forte was the conceptual planning and engineering, My work there was complete, so I left to join another nascent project in Indonesia: planning a sophisticated oil refinery in the jungles of Sumatra. That, too, presented a series of exciting challenges . . . but without the sometimes-frightening native cultures of PNG. The refinery was not constructed, largely because of political difficulties within Indonesia that were, at the time, undergoing some major upheavals within the country's longtime ruling class.[2]

Then came reassignment in 1990 to another major oil and gas project called Tengiz in Kazakhstan, which at the time was one of the socialist republics of the Soviet Union. Tengiz presented technical challenges of a different kind, and more complex political and managerial environments than I had ever experienced. A complex project even by Chevron's standards, the project had to contend with the government of the Soviet Union, which was on the verge of disintegrating. The Russians did not appreciate American companies playing in their backyard, and they erected all sorts of barriers. It was frustrating for everyone, mostly for the capital projects people of whom I was one. Yet we were able to accomplish some things. Responsible for project planning, I fleshed-out a major plan for the overall development based on what the Soviet national oil company had built thus far. We disbanded our group after about three years due to the political difficulties. Even so, Chevron was able to push the project though and produce and export oil, and it does so to this day.[3]

Next, I was assigned back to the PNG project, which by that time had been built just as we had planned it. Since first oil was extracted in 1992, the Kutubu oil field was producing nicely; Chevron and its partners were being rewarded handsomely for their investment.

Working with a clever attorney who specialized in mergers and acquisitions, we were charged with conceiving a way to commercialize all the gas that the field was producing.[4] Along with the PNG project partners, we conceptualized a pipeline to transport gas from the highlands of PNG to gas customers in far away Brisbane, Queensland, more than a thousand kilometers to the south. The concept was to deliver gas from the existing oil and gas facilities in the PNG Highlands through a new pipeline that would be parallel to the existing oil pipeline, traverse the Torres Strait, and run overland down the Queensland east coast to gas markets along the way. We would, however, have to deal with the PNG government and the still-restless natives of the PNG rainforest, and with the Australian and Queensland governments, the Aboriginal people of Far North Queensland, and the feared saltwater crocodile. After three years, a feasible project was planned and engineered, but exploration for additional gas reserve was disappointing. So the project was sold off to another of the gas field operators in the PNG Highlands. And my job was done.[5]

Retirement

A short time later, Chevron commenced what was euphemistically called "right-sizing." This meant a major reorganization of their operations, driven by depressed oil and gas prices, and a major realignment of business interests. Chevon had decided to exit PNG and was disbanding its operations in eastern Australia. The customary way of dealing with this was to offer those employees affected by the realignment generous severance packages. When offered to me, I immediately accepted their proposition. By then I was in my late 50s, and my family liked the idea of me being around, not off somewhere in the world working on a project in a remote land. So I took the early retirement package and happily didn't look back. That was in April 1999.

When I'd been at Stanford years earlier, one of my mentors was a professor named Hank Parker. Hank was a construction man with exceptional experience and keen intellect; he was a marvelous person with a splendid outlook on life. In my three years on campus, we became friends. One weekend during an excursion diving for abalone on the Northern California coast, Hank told some friends in our party—and me—that you've got opportunities in your lifetime for three separate professions. For him, it was fifteen years in heavy construction in places like South America, followed by fifteen years in academia (at Stanford), to be followed (hopefully) by fifteen years living in the White Mountains of New Hampshire. With this information, Hank was confiding that he planned to retire from Stanford in the coming year. He actually did just that and, along with his wife, he lived happily in the mountains for a long time, growing corn, chopping wood, and carrying water. He was a contented man living a useful life.

Back on that excursion of diving for abalone, Hank certainly got me thinking, which was one reason I joined an engineering company after Stanford. But leaving Chevron would be different—it meant I was about to enter phase three of the three-act life. Frankly, I found that terrifying. So, I committed to myself and my wife, Sharon, that I would build a life around multiple useful activities that involved both of us, and that, whatever they were, they would keep me home in Moraga, California. We both were well aware that, without a full plate of interesting and challenging things, I would not be happy, which would adversely affect both her and our children.

When a person with valuable skills becomes available—and is free of charge—it's not uncommon for someone with a need for help to come asking. No more than a week after I returned from Australia and PNG, my phone rang.

"Hi, Mike! This is Jay Tashiro, from the Town of Moraga. I hear you're available." I had never heard of this fellow.

"Who are you and how do you know that?"

"I'm the planning director for the town. We have a mutual friend."

I hate it when a conversation starts that way. He then revealed that the mutual friend was a fellow who had worked on my original PNG team years earlier, and that the friend was a planning commissioner for the town. A vacancy had opened on the planning commission and needed to be filled; our mutual friend thought I'd be a good fit. Next thing I knew, I was sitting before a subcommittee of two council members who were interviewing me to determine whether I was suitable for the appointment. The interview commenced with two gentlemen I had never met. It quickly became apparent they weren't one bit impressed by my credentials or my experience.

"You've been doing a lot of big things and working on large projects, but that's not what happens in Moraga. Very little happens here. And some of our citizens can be pretty tough on anyone who tries to do too much. They can be pretty loud and aggressive." My response to this put-down was simple:

"They can't be more terrifying that a savage PNG native who might love to knock me on the head or worse!"

That rejoinder took them aback and they offered me the job on the spot. A few days later (May 1999), I was sworn in by the town clerk and suddenly I was a planning commissioner for the Town of Moraga.

So much for fear of being idle. I had my work cut out for me.

Planning Commissioner

California cities are required to maintain a planning commission as part of city government. The Town of Moraga (which is legally labeled "The City of the Town of Moraga") is no exception. Planning commissions are intended to administer the land-use laws of the city. It's the Town Council that makes the laws. As such, the Planning Commission is a ministerial body, not legislative.

All cities are required to have a current General Plan which articulates the policies that regulate land use and a host of other things in the city. The General Plan is a city's constitution for land use and essentially describes how the town is meant to be developed and how it should be run. The plan can be extremely detailed and far-reaching in scope. Under state law it must be updated regularly (usually every ten years).

Planning commissions typically have seven citizen members who are appointed by the Town Council to terms of usually two years. The commission selects their chair, typically annually. The commission staff is the town's planning staff, led by the planning director, who reports to the town manager. Planning commissions meet twice monthly throughout the year. The Town of Moraga Planning Commission tends to be very busy, and its members are required to put in long hours preparing and attending public meetings and participating in subcommittee studies.

The commissions have many face-to-face encounters with the public. These meetings are called "hearings," and they provide an opportunity for the commissioners to hear the planning staff's reports and for the public to ask questions and comment. The primary subject matter is use of land within the town, and since most of the land in Moraga is owned by private citizens who want to do something with their land, the Planning Commission and the landowners often came to loggerheads over what was permitted and what was not. In its ministerial role, the commission also serves as a quasi-judicial body, ruling on the acceptability of land use proposals against the provisions of the plan's land-use ordinances. These encounters sometimes became contentious, and during my tenure the commission often found itself in an adversarial position relative to an aggrieved citizen. Citizens who opposed some proposed land use sometimes maintained that the town government was acting unfairly, perhaps even illegally; should a ruling seem unsatisfactory, the citizens were welcome to—and did—argue. Appeals to the Town Council were not unusual during my years on the commission, and the commission often found itself on opposite sides from members of the Town Council who sympathized with one party or other. The Town Council is an elected body, so its members tend to be influenced by their constituency; planning commissions, however, must strictly administer the law.

Because we worked with a number of different people, committees, and citizens—all of whom might have differing opinions and agendas—planning commissioners needed to employ a practiced finesse in order to reach decisions that were both legal and mutually acceptable. The fact that we had a good planning director was immensely helpful.

Perhaps the most challenging part of being a planning commissioner was serving as chair, which I was asked to do several times over a six-year period. Usually, running a smooth meeting was routine; people generally respected the process and didn't become unreasonable or disrespectful. However, there were instances when angry citizens became unruly. As chair, it was my duty to remain respectful of all persons, notwithstanding their behavior. Sometimes contentious discussions between commissioners ensued, and sometimes agreements were hard to reach. Yet, it was always imperative to steer the majority to reasonable conclusions. Sometimes it was like herding goats.

On a few occasions, the Town Council didn't agree with a decision of the commission, which resulted in an appeal directly to the council. As chair, I was brought before what felt like a hostile inquisition. One time the council overturned a commission decision—even though their reversal went counter to a clearly stated ordinance of the town. Their instructions to me were: "Try and be more flexible." Nonsense . . . change the ordinance if such flexibility is necessary.[6]

While serving on the Planning Commission, I did receive numerous positive remarks from citizens who had attended public hearings where things had become contentious. It was clear that they had noticed my behavior, and that they appreciated my sense of fairness.

In 2001, it was time for the town's General Plan to be updated. This is a major process and an opportunity to set right some things that clearly need fixing. An exceptional city planning consulting firm had been hired and a citizen committee had been formed, on which I was asked to serve as a planning commission representative. Most of the citizens on the committee were intelligent and thoughtful, and provided excellent contributions and common sense. Others were not so gifted. One of the Town Council representatives on the committee offered a shocking view: To him, the entire project was a waste of time because he believed the current 1990 General Plan was fine. But periodic updating was mandatory. Moreover, the committee had clearly demonstrated that the current plan was woefully out of date; it also failed to consider what could be done differently to create a better home for its 16,500 residents. What shocked me most was one of the goals of the 1990 plan, which the council insisted on retaining: "Maintain a minimum services government." That sounded like a prescription for doing nothing, the results of which could now be seen throughout the town. Notwithstanding those individuals and a few like-minded committee members, the new, successfully revised General Plan included many modifications and new policies that focused on a better future.[7]

Elected Council Member

During my later years on the Planning Commission, at least two town managers urged me to run for Town Council. They appreciated my approach and felt I could be a healthy addition. While flattered, I didn't take their urgings seriously, until one Town Council member, Mike Majchrzak, made it clear that I should run. Mike was a good friend and neighbor, and I appreciated his clear thinking on many issues. His urging was followed by encouraging advice from the town attorney, a woman whom I greatly respected and admired. So I agreed to "pull papers" in the summer of 2004 for the November election.

I had no idea what I should do to get elected, so I began by seeking advice from current and former council members. I heard several caveats: "Be careful not to make promises you don't know you'll be able to keep"; another, "Know the hot button issues and understand them well." But the most important tip came from a sage elder who admonished: "Know why you want to run. There are lots of 'electeds' who just want the job; you've got to want to DO the job."

So, having pulled papers to get on the ballot, I set out hiking the hills and valleys of Moraga, knocking on doors, and trying to engage with people. I was pleased to find almost everyone was willing to have a word about their concerns, letting me know what they thought ought to be done and, more important, what should not be done. It was eye-opening. But I don't recall many, if any, of them asking me what I wanted to accomplish. They didn't seem interested in my agenda. That surprised me, but I soon realized their reason.

Election day came and the votes showed that I clearly was the preferred candidate. My election, along with two other new faces on the political scene, was not even close. We were installed as members of the Moraga Town Council in December 2004.

As I settled into my new role, I came to know and understand the town staff. Previously, I knew the planning staff, but now there were departments for police, public works and engineering, parks and recreation, and administration and finance. All were led by the town manager. Several things were apparent. First, all departments were very small, considering their responsibilities; they were woefully understaffed. Second, several of the departments appeared to be going about their work in ad hoc ways; there was little of the orderly process I would have expected, even in the planning department. And third, there was an atmosphere of paucity. I heard constant lamenting that there were no funds to do things that should be done; worse, there was little urgency to do much of anything. I concluded that this attitude reflected a culture of scarcity which caused the staff to be negative and just say "no" instead of "let me see if we can do that." One staff person remarked to me one day that this reflected that Moraga has a "minimum services government." Even the town manager seemed to accept this negativity. I sure didn't.

The next thing I discovered about town staff is that, notwithstanding the obvious shortcomings of their situations, many of them didn't appreciate interference by elected town officials. Sometimes merely asking a probing question sparked a subtle indignation. They were the professionals; they did the work. While none of them ever went so far as to say "Butt out!" their feelings were oftentimes palpable. The problem was, not much was being done, nor could it be. Expectations from the Town Council at that time did not seem high. Certainly, councils in those days did not want to pay for much, or find ways to fund new things.

The bright side was the citizens. It was clear that much of what had been happening in the town was due to citizen volunteers. Citizens volunteered for all manner of service clubs, committees, and commissions. They did so with impressive enthusiasm, in many instances with terrific results. Indeed, some citizens groups were doing things that in many other cities were being done by the city staff—for instance, organizing and producing the annual summer concert series at Moraga Commons. Citizen groups happily jumped in and carried the day, operating in their own ad hoc ways. It seemed to work.

Through my twelve years on the Town Council, I was selected to be mayor by my colleagues three times. For some mayors, the one-year terms are customarily ceremonial, not much else. But I didn't operate that way. There was no reason why important things couldn't get done, provided there was leadership and encouragement. It was evident to me, and to some others, what a few of those important things were. And it was abundantly clear that town staff and willing volunteers could get much more done if they were effectively motivated. The council needed a shift in attitude, the staff needed some serious upgrading both in terms of personnel and procedure, and citizen volunteers needed continual encouragement to participate in making good things happen. But it was obvious that nothing could get done without broad public support. It was essential to appreciate what truly mattered to Moragans, to know their special interests, and to recognize what they did not want. In other words, Moragans' values needed to be clearly understood. There was so much that could be done with imagination and perseverance. In 2005, it seemed to me that it was time to get moving on things.

But what my wild-eyed imagination could not foresee were the difficulties that I, and like-minded Moragans, would encounter. It quickly became abundantly clear that in Moraga, as in so many places, people are driven by their own interests. Little else matters. Their politics are driven by things close to home. In short, their politics is local. And that's how the game had to be played in order to get anything done.

CHAPTER 2

What Tip O'Neill Meant

"ALL POLITICS IS LOCAL." That aphorism is attributed to Tip O'Neill, a long-serving former Speaker of the House in the U.S. Congress. But who was this man and what did he really mean? And how important is local politics? Do local politics rather than national politics dominate the political landscape? Before turning directly to the Town of Moraga, which is the focus of my adventures in local politics, let's see what we can learn from examining the past.

The Boston Politician

Thomas Phillip "Tip" O'Neill Jr. (1912-1994) was a Democratic politician from Massachusetts who served in the U.S. House of Representatives from 1952 until 1987, representing Cambridge, which is adjacent to Boston. He was Speaker of the House from 1977 to 1987, the longest uninterrupted tenure of anyone to hold that position. During his storied years, he became an American legend, admired by many, even by numerous of his political foes. He was a large man in physical stature, even larger in personality. Even people like my father, a lifelong and die-hard Republican, thought highly of Tip O'Neill. As a young man growing up in the Boston area, I was aware of Tip, and I admired him as well. Who couldn't?

Tip O'Neill was a product of the Great Depression and was a devoted New Dealer of the Franklin Delano Roosevelt mold. He represented North Cambridge, home to many not-very-well-off Irish Catholics. His political creed held that government's role was to help those in need, a belief structure that endured throughout his political career. Perhaps the reason he came to be revered by so many is that he honestly believed in what he said and did; he could be counted on to do things for the people he represented. And for that he was re-elected, almost always unopposed, time and again over his thirty-five-year career in Congress.

O'Neill studied at Boston College, a parochial college in the Boston suburbs, and graduated in 1936. As early as 1928, at age fifteen, he was campaigning for Al Smith in that year's presidential race. His political activism continued during his time at Boston College. During his senior year, he ran for a seat on the Cambridge City Council, which he lost by a mere 160 votes. As Tip himself explained, he lost because he took his own neighborhood (Cambridge) for granted. He related that his father later advised him that "All politics is local. Don't forget it." He never did, and he never lost another election.[1]

Tip O'Neill served in Congress for a very long time. Yet he recognized when it was time to retire. He did not run for re-election after some eighteen terms in Congress and retired gracefully to Boston. He knew when it was time to leave.

Tip O'Neill, ca. 1975.
Mikki Ansin/Getty Images

His Aphorism

What was Tip O'Neill's key to political success? Simple. He cared about the people he represented; he did things in their interest. In his political memoirs, O'Neill tells his life story in and out of politics, and reveals his beliefs and the political instincts that made him so successful.[2] And in his short book *All Politics Is Local*, he provides lots of advice to those readers he presumes are interested in politics, and he explains what he meant by the simple aphorism.[3] Introducing that book O'Neill says, "This book is a primer on politics, or at least politics as practiced in my sixty years of experience." He offers plenty of good advice, including:

> A politician learns that if a constituent calls about a problem, even if it's about a streetlight, you don't tell them to call City Hall. You call City Hall. . . . Pay attention to [your] own backyard and take care of [your] folks. Get home often and report to [your] constituents. Keep them informed and you will find that they will like and respect you and allow you to be a "national" [c]ongressman and vote for the things that are good for the country but may not have a direct impact on your district. . . . It's better if you can say you voted a certain way because it was "good for the economy of the area," but you don't always have that reason. . . . This is what I mean when I say, "All politics is local."[4]

From that introduction, O"Neill launches into a series of anecdotes, which he calls "Rules of the Game." These are folksy tales, each with a lesson he suggests contributes to effective governing. Most are written in less than five-hundred words; they are right to the point. They form what O'Neill calls a "handbook" for other politicians. From his portfolio of tales, there are some choice nuggets:

> "In a campaign, get volunteers involved. . . . When we opened a campaign headquarters, we would immediately recruit as many volunteers as we could. . . . [Regardless of what they were asked to do] they would go home and tell their friends and neighbors that they were 'working in Tip O'Neill's campaign'."[5]

> "Keep your speeches short. . . . [An audience's attention span is about eighteen minutes.] . . . I set my watch at sixteen minutes and after it goes off, I wind up in two."[6]

> "You can switch a position, but do it quickly and openly. . . . Tell [your constituents] the truth. . . . Come clean about it, and do it quickly. Issue a statement saying you were convinced by one set of arguments, but now that you've had a chance to hear the other side, you believe your earlier position was mistaken."[7]

> "In politics, no chore is too small. . . . The tendency is nowadays for mass appeal, mass mailings, and mass media. But if you don't do the little things, none of this 'mass' business is going to work. . . . I used to send letters of condolence to widows in my district. I got their names from the funeral notices."[8]

> "Getting elected doesn't mean they love you forever. . . . Leadership brings with it the people who love to put you on a pedestal so they can throw brickbats and mud at you."[9]

> "Go with the pros—and train some new ones. . . . Hire some professional help. . . . Good staff can make a difference."[10]

> "Keep your perspective. . . . Take your job seriously but don't take yourself seriously."[11]

"It's easier to run for office than to run the office. . . . In a campaign the candidate raises expectations and convinces the voters he or she can walk on water. That's what the whole effort is about. . . . Then comes the time to deliver."[12]

"Know when to quit. . . . If you get frustrated over a long period of time or find yourself getting cynical or find yourself hiding from your voters or your colleagues, it's time to get out."[13]

Some of O'Neill's political tips that resonate:[14]

"It's a round world—what goes around, comes around."

"You can accomplish anything if you're willing to let someone else take the credit."

"Never lose your idealism."

"Lead by consent not by demand."

"Learn to say, 'I don't know but I will find out.'"

"Don't stay mad—there's always tomorrow. Today's enemy is tomorrow's ally."

"Tell the truth the first time and you don't have to remember what you said."

Service to Constituents

In his analysis of the principle that "All Politics Is Local," political scientist Andrew Gelman takes issue with Tip O'Neill. Gelman comments on the debate over whether all politics are, indeed, local, or rather national in character. He begins by citing a Wikipedia explanation of the aphorism as follows:

Politicians must appeal to the simple, mundane and everyday concerns of those who elect them into office. Those personal issues, rather than the big and intangible ideas, are often what voters care most about, according to this principle.[15]

Gelman then joins the debate over whether a politician's success results more from the service delivered to constituents, or from the gerrymandering of the political districts the politician represents. His view is that "all the constituent service in the world won't stop you from getting gerrymandered."[16] He posits that O'Neill came from a "safe" district in a thoroughly Democratic district outside Boston, and that his seat was continually secure by virtue of shifting district lines that helped ensure his electorate. This seems like a cynical view, as it minimizes the importance of satisfying popular appeal related to a politician's exceptional service to constituents. Gelman insists that politicians like Tip O'Neill maintain their power by remaining on good terms with the powers in their states. Yet he provides no persuasive argument resolution, at least in my mind. To me, service to constituents is all important.

Local and National Politics

Politics is the art of getting people to go along with what you want,
when otherwise they may not.

That was spoken by a professor in a political science lecture I was auditing at the University of Pennsylvania. It was in the 1960s, and I was an undergraduate student, but even then, it made sense to me. It still does now. And it applies to both local and national levels. What I find peculiar is that within the political science community there appears to be a debate over the relative stature of local politics vis-à-vis national politics. Perhaps I am missing something, but it seems to me that the local political arena drives the political inclinations of more people than at other levels. Political scientist Jessica Trounstine maintains that "local politics has been relegated to the periphery of political science and many explanations have been offered for the marginalization of the subfield."[17] While she doesn't provide new insights that help settle the debate, she does make some interesting points. In her final analysis she simply encourages more study of local politics: "Research on local politics can and should contribute to broader debates in political science and ensure that we understand both how and why cities are unique."[18]

Trounstine also cites numerous reasons why city politics are much less important than national politics. She points to increased media attention on national issues, and a sense that there is no urban crisis, that nothing important happens in the cities according to this wisdom, only at the national level. She maintains that the federal system constrains city decision-making, so that cities are no longer free to govern themselves. These conceits certainly paint a grim picture of local politics. However, local politics are important and, as she herself says, "local contexts shape state and national politics." Trounstine adds that as of 1992, there were some 340,000 members of local governing boards representing nearly 85,000 different governmental units, compared with the federal level where there were 535 legislators serving a single governmental unit, and nearly 7,400 state legislators in the 50 states. Moreover, local elections are held with greater frequency than federal or state elections, which suggests that voters are more involved at local levels than one might realize. Despite gradual aggregation of political power at federal and state levels over recent decades, Trounstine maintains there is a current trend toward devolution to local levels. This suggests that local politics are increasingly important. And public opinion surveys demonstrate that what concerns local voters most are local issues like education, crime, and land use.[19]

To maintain that local issues are not important seems elitist and nonsensical. Local issues are important—perhaps not glamorous, maybe mundane, but nonetheless important. In the Town of Moraga, Town Council members are elected at large. Party affiliation has little or no bearing on the political contests. For sure, some ultra-partisan citizens might be aware of a candidate's party preference and use that as a criterion for whether they feel the candidate is suitable. But this brand of partisanship is minor stacked against a candidate's prospects for delivering on what is promised, or a track record for having done so. In my experience, the politics in a place like Moraga are driven by local issues, and that's where a wise Moraga politician needs to pay attention. Tip O'Neill was on the mark, in my view, when he said: *All Politics Is Local*.

A good example of that statement is the Town of Moraga and its neighboring cities within the Lamorinda region in Contra Costa County, California.[20]

CHAPTER 3

Rancho Laguna de
los Palos Colorados

ALOOK INTO THE HISTORY of the Town of Moraga—where things political are
definitely local—sheds a great deal of light on the character of the modern-day
community and helps explain why Moraga politics are what they have become. This is
greatly facilitated by a good book written by Sandy Kimball and published by the Moraga
Historical Society entitled *Moraga's Pride: Rancho Laguna de los Palos Colorados*. The book
offers a readable story (accompanied by excellent illustrations) and explains Moraga's
history and character.[1]

Moraga is a small town nestled in the valleys south of present-day Highway 24,
approximately 5 miles equidistant from the cities of Orinda (to the northwest) and Lafayette
(on the north), and about 6 miles from Walnut Creek (on the northeast). Moraga is remote
with limited ways into and out of the town, which is why it is commonly referred to as a
"cul-de-sac" community. The geographical separateness of the three cities from the rest of
Contra Costa County contributes to the opinion shared by many that the three communities
are culturally different than the rest of the County.[2]

Early Settlers

Moraga was once the territory of Indigenous peoples from several tribes spread over coastal
northern California. For hundreds of years, these Native Americans lived in small groups
throughout a vast area from the coast eastward into the inland valleys. They engaged in
subsistence farming, some hunting, and foraging. They were peaceful people. But when
Europeans arrived by sea and contact was made, European diseases ravaged the tribes,
wiping out nearly 90 percent of the Indigenous population.[3]

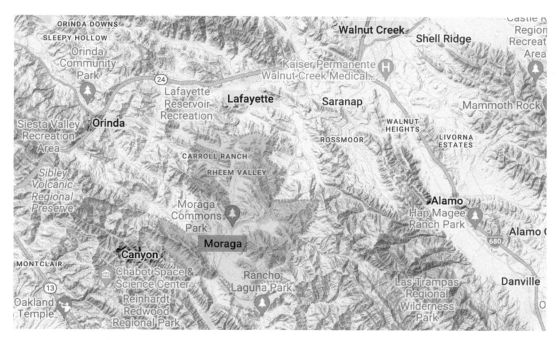

Lamorinda Area Map: Highlighting Moraga, Orinda, Lafayette, Canyon, and Walnut Creek. (North is shown at top of map.) Based on Google MapGIS, 2024.

When the Spanish arrived in the Bay Area in 1769, they established missions (Carmel, Fremont, San Francisco, and others). Soon thereafter, Spanish exploration parties led by Juan Bautista de Anza and others reached inland east of San Francisco Bay into what became known as Contra Costa. Among de Anza's confederates was Joseph (Jose) Joaquin Moraga, who explored the Bay area extensively during the 1770s. Jose Joaquin Moraga is credited with establishment of the San Francisco presidio and Mission Delores.

Under the new Mexican government, the Spanish king granted land to soldiers who were loyal to Spain, including Jose Joaquin's grandson Joaquin Moraga. In lieu of unpaid wages, Moraga—a soldier in the king's army like his father and grandfather—received approximately 13,400 acres of land. The grant land was named Rancho Laguna de los Palos Colorados. Joaquin Moraga is thereby credited with founding what became known as Moraga in the late 1700s.[4]

Joaquin's descendants settled within the Rancho Laguna grant. They built the Moraga Adobe in the 1840s as a family residence. Located on a hill overlooking the valley lands where cattle grazed, the home was a small, single-story building with thick adobe walls and a timber roof. The original edifice had but three rooms, until lean-to additions expanded that number and provided an attic, which served as a loft. Members of the immediate family lived at the Adobe, or close by. By 1850, the Adobe had become a place for happy occasions called "fandangos," and it remained a lively house where the Moragas often gathered until the 1880s.[5]

Around 1880, the Moraga family began selling off portions of the vast rancho territory. Speculators were aware of the rancho and they pursued the family about acquiring portions of the lands. Most notorious of them was Horace Carpentier, a New York opportunist. Carpentier was persistent and managed to buy out the remaining Moraga family members, whereupon he installed his own rancho manager. The Moraga Adobe was occupied thereafter by renters who worked on the rancho lands for Carpentier's operation. For a while after 1890, the Adobe was abandoned, and it deteriorated from exposure and damage when it became a den for feral hogs.[6]

When gold had been depleted after the Gold Rush of 1848-49, hordes of newcomers flooded into Northern California and the rancho. Numerous land transactions were completed, and by 1878, the original Mexican families (that is, the Moragas and Bernals) had been displaced by Carpentier. In 1885, when he closed a deal with Moraga heirs for the remaining Moraga parcels within the rancho, he was the virtual sole owner of rancho land.[7]

Most of the newcomers to the rancho squatted on vacant land, many of them becoming Moraga's first families. Some were lumberjacks who timbered the redwood forest on the south side of the rancho (present-day Canyon); some farmed the land and raised livestock; others built substantial ranches. Not all was peaceful amongst these folks; there were quarrels and encroachments on one another. One notable episode in the late 1870s resulted in the so-called "Moraga War," which erupted over a fence that was erected on a neighbor's alleged property and resulted in some loss of life and property damage. However, by 1886, the ranches had been bought by Carpentier and the era of the ranchers was ended.[8] Carpentier's rancho land now became tenant lands. Ranchers who had formerly worked the land became the tenants who rented from Carpentier.

Land Barons

By 1889, Carpentier had sold all his ranch lands to other investors. Two of them—named Williamson and Grant—had previous connections with the railroads in California; they bought 13,316 acres of the rancho and formed the Moraga Land Company, with the intention to subdivide the land into town lots and small ranches. Their plan included a railroad spur from the California and Nevada Railway, which would extend south from current-day El Sobrante to the Orinda Crossroads (Bryant Station), and then proceed south to the present-day Moraga Center. Williamson and Grant widely publicized their plan in an effort to attract prospective homeowners from the San Francisco area. However, the plan failed. Only a few lots were developed and, although the right-of-way had been prepared, no rails were laid between Orinda and Moraga.[9]

Moraga Land Company continued to acquire land within the rancho, and, by 1913, virtually all the rancho land was back in the hands of a sole owner: this time, James Irvine. Irvine was a land developer and ranch owner from Southern California.[10] He called his new operation the Moraga Company, and his emphasis was on agriculture and, to a lesser extent, on development. The center of the Moraga Company's agribusiness was at the Moraga Ranch, which exists to present-day in the Moraga Center. In time, Moraga became the largest producer of pears in the world. The Oakland & Antioch Railway was completed in 1913, passing through the Moraga Center, which by then included a store and a hotel (present-day Moraga Barn). Agricultural emphasis was heightened over the ensuing years once a rail link to Oakland opened markets for Moraga products.

Moraga Station, looking northward along present-day Viader Drive, ca. 1927. At left, Moraga Barn; at center, station and freight loading; at right, Sacramento Northern Railway line (east bound). Sally Kimball, Moraga's Pride: Rancho Laguna de los Palos Colorados, *2nd ed. (1987; Moraga, Calif.: Moraga Historical Society, 2002), 113.*

Irvine's sales manager was Robert Burgess, who cooked up plans for prospective communities within the rancho lands. Now that rail service to Oakland and San Francisco was operating, land development could resume. Burgess was a promoter, installing massive advertising signs in the Moraga area that shouted "Watch Moraga Grow/Live Here/Work in the City." Promotional headquarters were established in 1914 in a building next to the Moraga Hotel, adjacent to the depot for the O&A railroad (later to be absorbed into the Sacramento Northern Railway). In 1927, the Moraga Company offered land to Saint Mary's College and what was then called College of the Holy Names (now Holy Names University), which at that time were both located in Oakland. Saint Mary's took the offer, and the present Saint Mary's College was built. (In 1928, Saint Mary's relocated to Moraga; Holy Names remained in Oakland.) By 1936, as the country was emerging from the Great

Depression, demand for housing was accelerating, and Irvine realized that developing the land was more profitable than selling parcels. He therefore reoriented the Moraga Company toward community development, his intention being for Moraga to become a bedroom community. Then agriculture began a steep decline.[11]

In 1916, Gertrude Mallete and Alberta Higgins bought 20 acres of land from a descendant of the Lucas family, one of the landowners in vicinity of present-day Rheem Center, located 2 miles north of the Moraga Center. They erected a Spanish-style building for an orphanage, which is the present-day Hacienda de las Flores (now owned by Town of Moraga and best known as a venue for weddings). The orphanage was shut down by the State of California, whereupon the two women attempted to farm the land. That wasn't successful. Donald Rheem bought the property in 1934 as a summer home. He added a second story, expanded the grounds, and added a five-car garage (present-day "La Casita"), a residential housing development, a pool, cabaña with movie theater (present-day "Pavilion"), a racetrack, and stables. It was quite something. From 1944 to 1947, Rheem bought additional Moraga Company lands, totaling 1,650 acres. He envisaged subdivisions, including what is now the Rheem Valley Shopping Center, which he started to build in 1954.[12]

The Developers

Donald Rheem's ownership spelled the end of sole ownership of rancho lands, which had been the case since the days of the Moragas and the Bernals. Now there were two developers: the Moraga Company and Donald Rheem. It seemed that the rancho was poised for major new development. After James Irvine died in 1947, the Moraga Company directors proposed that Rheem become sole stockholder of the Moraga Company. But that plan was thwarted owing to disagreements within the Moraga Company board. The Moraga Company then found a buyer, Utah Construction and Mining Company, which had major land development interests.[13] Donald Rheem left the Moraga scene in 1973, when he sold the Rheem Center to Dohemann Development Company.[14]

Utah developed grandiose plans for a model community of 28,000 residents on over 5,000 acres of rancho land. The plan included parks, shopping centers, and churches. Open zoning would be allowed for light industry, retail, even a lumberyard. Moraga residents were horrified. The County Planning Commission was inundated with protests, which, in 1954, prompted the county supervisors to form an emergency committee—comprised of representatives from Moraga, Orinda, and Concord—for the purpose of developing a General Plan. The committee also served as a "watchdog" on the County Planning Department (as it was called back then). Under such oversight, the first General Plan for Moraga was produced in 1962.

The General Plan called for considerably less housing than proposed by Utah. But Utah didn't seem to get the message, for within three years they proposed to add a country club and a swim and tennis club, and they increased commercial uses in the Rheem Center area. Moraga citizens' reactions prompted the formation of yet another General Plan study committee, this one including county staff, Utah representatives, and only Moraga representatives. A revision to the plan was produced in 1969 that reduced Utah's proposal to what was more acceptable to Moragans, who wanted a more residential community.[15]

During the 1960s, Utah responded to a huge rush of home-buying interest by engaging the Moraga Company to handle subdivision work and sell finished lots to individual builders. "From 1955 to 1965, thirty-one subdivisions were developed and homesites were sold to twenty builders. During those ten years, Utah owned the rancho, [but Utah] never built a single house."[16]

A new developer on the scene was Russell Bruzzone, who began his Moraga career subdividing and building in Burton Valley. He bought the Moraga Center in 1964 from Utah, who had designed the center but never did anything more. Bruzzone proceeded to construct what would be the second shopping center in Moraga, just a few miles south of the Rheem Center, no doubt on the presumption that significantly more "rooftops" would be built. In 1967, he purchased Utah's remaining rancho land (2,300 acres), on which he built the Moraga Country Club and Camino Ricardo subdivisions. He actively pursued expansions of those subdivisions until he died in 2001.[17]

By 1972, the number of developed tracts and dramatic disappearance of open space concerned Maraga citizens and reignited talks about incorporation of the town. "There had been some talk of incorporating the area since the early 1960s as residents realized that the lack of local control could prove a threat to their country lifestyle." Incorporation came swiftly in November 1974.[18]

One of Utah's last land sales was the property opposite Campolindo High School, which was sold to Richland Development Corporation. Richland designed a plan to build 146 single family homes plus an 18-hole golf course on 460 acres of former cattle grazing land. The proposed development caused a major uproar and became the subject of extensive legal wrangling for some thirty years. To date, construction of the project, even though approved by the Town of Moraga, has yet to begin.[19]

Rancho Communities

As Moraga was developing, so were other communities within the rancho: Lafayette, Orinda, Canyon, and Redwood. Canyon and Redwood were called "sobrante" communities; they were on land outside the boundaries of the rancho, but their inhabitants were culturally tied to those communities within the rancho. Redwood was on the south end of the valley that is now San Leandro Reservoir; the town was acquired by eminent domain by EBMUD in 1927 and, after the San Leandro Dam was built to create the reservoir, was inundated by rising reservoir waters. Canyon, known originally as "Sequoya," became a small outlying settlement set apart from Moraga, and was home to nature lovers, many of whom worked in San Francisco. Other sobrante lands included Gateway, Valle Vista, Indian Valley, and the hills east of Moraga that extended over Las Trampas ridge.[20]

Lafayette, situated on the northeast corner of Moraga Rancho, was settled in 1853. By 1900, the center of the community was a vibrant place, and in 1914, the town hall was built (present-day Town Playhouse). Lafayette's growth was largely determined by the rail and roadway systems that reached the town after 1920: the Oakland, Antioch & Eastern Railway, and the Caldecott Tunnel and Highway 24 corridor. These transportation services allowed new residents to flow into the area from Oakland and San Francisco. After unsuccessful attempts to incorporate in 1959, Lafayette citizens voted to incorporate their community into a city in 1968.[21]

How did the town come by its name? It didn't happen quickly. Previously, it had been known as Dog Town, Brown's Corner, Centerville, and Acalanus (the name of the initial Mexican land grant). When Benjamin Shreve became the town's first postmaster in 1857, he favored Centerville, but that name was already taken by another California town. So Shreve went with his second choice, La Fayette. This was changed finally to Lafayette in honor of the French general who participated in the American Revolutionary War.[22]

Orinda, on the northwest corner of the Moraga Rancho, originally was a summer retreat for San Franciscans and Oaklanders. It became an attractive destination when the California and Nevada Railroad provided rail services from Emeryville south to Bryant Station at Orinda Crossroads at the center of Orinda Village. The El Sobrante portion of modern Orinda was built up north of present-day Highway 24; the southern portion was culturally part of Moraga but became part of Orinda owing to the school district's schemes for allocating students (details of this later). Orinda was settled year-round by young families seeking a country lifestyle. Incorporation as a city was defeated in 1967, but ultimately was approved by voters in 1985.[23]

And the name Orinda? Oddly, it doesn't follow the Spanish naming scheme found throughout much of the Bay Area. But apparently, in 1876, the wife of the town's sheriff, Alice Mars Cameron, was particularly fond of a seventeenth-century English poet named Katherine Fowler Phillips. Phillips was called "Matchless Orinda." It's said that, for this reason, Alice named her home "Orinda." In 1920, Orinda became the name of the town.[24]

Comparatively speaking, Moraga's etymology is more straightforward: Moraga simply follows from the name of the town's founder, Joaquin Moraga.

Moraga and its surrounding neighbors are collectively known as "Lamorinda." The name is a blend word from the names of the three cities that make up the region: Lafayette,

Moraga, and Orinda.[25] As of 2010, the three cities had a combined population of 57,552, with Lafayette having the largest population (24,000) and Moraga the smallest (16,500). The tri-cities are recognized as relatively affluent, and Lamorindans are considered by themselves and some others to be well-educated. The Lamorinda communities are recognized for their exceptional schools; Lafayette is the commercial center, Orinda is more rural, and Moraga is known for its expansive open space, agricultural heritage, and St. Mary's College. The three cities are regarded as a cultural bloc by the other sixteen Contra Costa County cities.

The Lamorinda cities have always coexisted and will probably continue to do so in the future. Yet there are contentious issues that have been serious at times and will no doubt become prominent in the future. The most significant conflicts are related to growth and the impacts that any development in one city has on the others. The issue usually is traffic. Since Moraga is a cul-de-sac community and intercity traffic flows to and from Moraga through the other two cities, Moraga usually becomes the focus of criticism. For instance, the major issue surrounding the Palos Colorados development project was traffic impacts.[26] Any Moraga development draws extra scrutiny from Lafayette, a bit less so from Orinda. But if either Lafayette or Orinda do anything that disrupts the traffic flow through their cities, and Moragans are adversely impacted, Moragans usually complain vigorously. Sometimes things can become quite heated. Notwithstanding such moments, both Lafayette and Orinda should realize that Moraga has done them both huge favors in the past related to rail and highway developments that affect all of Lamorinda. (Perhaps they have, since in the past 10-15 years, relationships between the three cities seem to have improved a bit.)

Railways—The Sacramento Northern

As we have seen, the rancho was a very large and sparsely settled territory where livestock and agriculture were the principal focus. Moraga was remote; access from Orinda and Lafayette was challenging. Important railroad and highway projects opened the access to Moraga and resulted in immense changes to the once remote rancho. And the access posed threats to the citizens of all three Lamorinda communities.

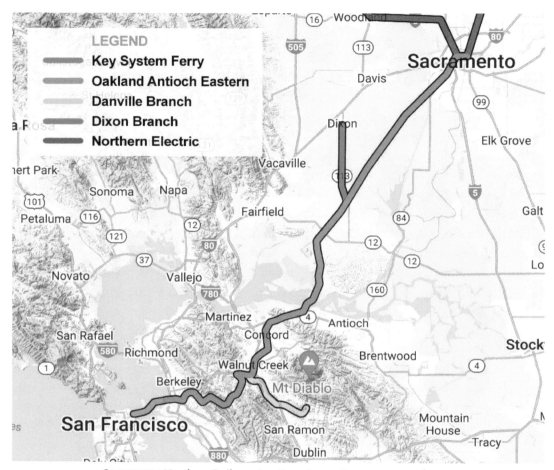

Sacramento Northern Railway, San Francisco to Sacramento as of 1920.
Based on Google Map, GIS and Demoro, 168-90. Annotation by author.

With interurban railway developments in the early 1900s, things began to change for towns like Moraga. Attempts during the closing years of the nineteenth century to push rail service from Emeryville through Orinda and on to Moraga never materialized; as noted earlier, rail service was completed as far as Bryant Station in Orinda, but the rails were never constructed to Moraga. It wasn't until 1913, when the Oakland, Antioch & Eastern (OA&E) Railway bored a 3,200-foot-long tunnel through the Oakland Hills at Shepherd Canyon, that rail service reached the Moraga Rancho. For forty-four years thereafter, the railroad was the lifeblood for Moraga, providing the only viable way to move freight and people through the Moraga Valley west to Oakland and San Francisco, and east to Walnut Creek and beyond.

The OA&E was an "interurban" railway that ran an all-electric train from Emeryville to Sacramento. Passengers would catch a Key System ferry at the San Francisco ferry terminal for a short passage across the bay to the Key terminal offshore of Emeryville. The Key System owned a long pier on which OA&E cars traveled to pick up passengers for the onward trip eastward.[27] (See accompanying maps.) The train then proceeded through Oakland past Temescal and south along present-day Highway 13 to present-day Montclair on the west face of the 900-foot-high Oakland Hills. There the rails proceeded upgrade along Shepherd Canyon Road to a station called Havens, which was the west portal of the 3,200-foot-long tunnel that was bored under Skyline Blvd., which runs along the Oakland Hills ridgeline. From the east portal (Eastport), the rails followed Pinehurst Road down to present-day Canyon, where there was a station. The rails then went north along present-day Canyon Road, past Valle Vista, crossed the south boundary of the present-day Moraga Country Club, and curved left onto present-day Augusta Drive before reaching Railroad Avenue (now Viader Drive). Trains stopped at Moraga Station, where there were passenger and freight loading facilities, and where the Moraga Barn (which was operated as a hotel) was subsequently established. The rails then proceeded northeasterly across the present-day Moraga Center, through the present-day Moraga Commons, and along the present-day Lafayette-Moraga Trail on the way toward Burton Valley.[28]

About a mile farther along, the rails veered east toward the site of St. Mary's College, which was constructed in 1928. A station was built at the college to serve students and faculty commuters. The rails then proceeded to eastern Lafayette and followed a sweeping route northwest to Lafayette center, before turning east toward Reliez Station, where there was another station. The route then proceeded out present-day Olympic Blvd to Saranap. A spur line extended service from Saranap south through Danville and out to Diablo station in the Diablo foothills. From Saranap, the line went through Walnut Creek, Concord, and on to Pittsburg. The rails stopped at a ferry terminal west of Antioch on the south shore of the Sacramento River opposite Chipps Island. A ferry transported trains across the river landing on Montezuma Slough before proceeding along the river levees to Sacramento. When the railway was fully operating, the trip from San Francisco to Sacramento took three-and-a-half hours.

Sacramento Northern Railway, Moraga Train Station. At center, motorcoach and passenger car; at right, the station and Moraga Barn, 1950. Susan K. Skilton, Images of America: Moraga *(Charleston, S.C.: Arcadia Publishing, 2016), 23. Photo by J. G. Graham, courtesy of Bay Area Electric Railroad Association, Western Railway Museum archives.*

Sacramento Northern Railway, St. Mary's station. At left, motorcoach and passenger car; at center, the station; at right, St. Mary's College chapel, 1941. Sandy Kimball, Moraga's Pride: Rancho Laguna de los Palos Colorado, *2nd ed. (1987; Moraga, California: Moraga Historical Society, 2002), 182.*

The OA&E operated for fifteen years over this route, providing both passenger and freight service to all the communities along the way. Another interurban system called the Northern Electric Railway (NE) ran between Sacramento to Colusa and Chico to the north, and also Woodland to the west. In 1928, the NE merged with the OA&E to become the Sacramento Northern Railway (SN). When the merged system was operating, the SN provided a 185-mile-long, all-electric rail system between Chico and Oakland. The last passenger service on the OA&E was in 1941; the last freight was carried in 1957.[29]

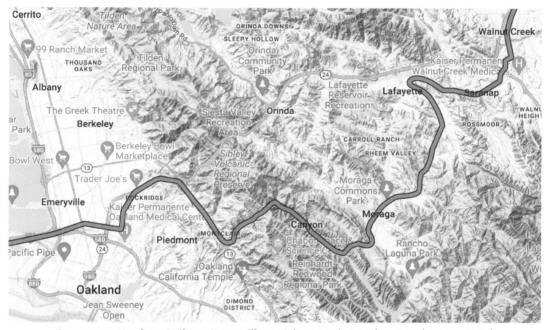

Sacramento Northern Railway, Emeryville to Walnut Creek. Based on Google MapGIS and Demoro, 168-90. Annotation by author.

Moraga was a major beneficiary of this service; Lafayette's growth was definitely boosted by the rail service penetrating the town's southeasterly parts. Orinda did not directly benefit from the SN interurban system.

Motor observation railcar Moraga carrying "The Comet" drumhead. This observation car is shown operating on the line through the Oakland Hills, Calif., 1915. Passengers would enjoy the ride on the open platform, viewing the scenery as the train passed through the countryside. Photo by W. J. Bullus, Vernon Sappers Collection, Demoro, 84.

Caldecott Tunnel and the Highway 24 Corridor

No highway development has had as much impact on Contra Costa County—in particular, Lamorinda—as the Highway 24 corridor and the Caldecott Tunnel. Other than the railroad tunnel at Shepherd Canyon, the only attempt to penetrate the Oakland Hills had been in the 1870s, when a project was launched to bore the Kennedy Tunnel near the Claremont Hotel. But the project was abandoned for lack of funding. Later, the Contra Costa Tunnel was built and opened to limited vehicular traffic in 1903. A single-lane passage, it crossed the hills just 320 feet below the summit, but it had dangerously steep approaches. Moreover, the tunnel was a marginal affair. By 1928, when population pressures in the new communities in Contra Costa County had become severe, a roadway through the Oakland Hills was justified. This was the twin-bore Caldecott Tunnel, which opened in 1937. A third bore was completed in 1964, and a fourth bore was opened in 2013.[30] Since opening the first bore, traffic and freight has flowed reasonably freely both east (Contra Costa County) and west

(Alameda County). Highway 24 in Contra Costa County clearly had been built with future growth and expansion in mind.

The Highway 24 corridor included the Bay Area Rapid Transit (BART) train service, which runs through its own tunnel parallel to the Caldecott Tunnel, and down the centerline of Highway 24. First proposed in 1953 as the solution to Contra Costa traffic problems, the rail service took twelve years to complete. While certainly providing much faster transportation from Orinda and Lafayette to San Francsico, BART has never come close to solving Bay Area traffic congestion. Nonetheless, early on, the benefits to those living in Lamorinda were many, as commuting to and from San Francisco made suburban living in Lamorinda much more appealing.

Highway 24 (and BART) certainly provided an efficient transportation corridor, but the corridor bifurcated the rancho communities of Orinda and Lafayette into north and south. Orinda was especially impacted since the center of the city—the area known as Orinda Crossroads—was split into two villages. A lesser impact was experienced by Lafayette since the corridor passed to the north of the commercial center. Moraga escaped any such adverse impacts. Nonetheless, the corridor did open all three communities to new traffic, which helped promote development in all three. Without question, improved transportation helped swell the population of Lamorinda to over 57,000 people, but at a cost. Such dramatic development threatened the lifestyle of many of those who moved to the area seeking a "semirural" environment. The struggles presented by the pro-growth people supporting development versus those wishing to preserve open space came to dominate the politics of Lamorinda, particularly in Moraga.

Freeways Through Moraga

Since the early days of Moraga development in the 1920s, the idea of roadways sweeping through Moraga and the two adjacent cities was a splendid prospect for developers. Not so for those who wanted to preserve the smallness of their rural communities. From the earliest days of the Moraga Rancho, rudimentary roads crisscrossed the Moraga Valley. Most were mere paths passable by horse and cart, providing access to the settlements and ranches that were scattered throughout the valleys. Some routes had commercial purposes as they attempted to provide avenues for logging and agricultural products to reach markets. But for a long while, sturdy roads were never built, until four roadways of consequence were developed: Moraga Road, Moraga Way, Canyon Road, and St. Mary's Road.[31]

Several other roadway projects were not built as planned. Had they been completed, they would have dramatically changed Moraga, and not necessarily for the better. But three projects were particularly prominent, and they played important roles in Moraga's political relationships with other Lamorinda cities.

Bollinger Canyon Road

In the early days, a primitive trail led from what would become St. Mary's Road in the Moraga Valley (east of St. Mary's College campus), along Las Trampas Creek, over Las Trampas Ridge, and down into the San Ramon Valley. The creek formed Bollinger Canyon, which was named for a rancher who operated on the San Ramon side of Las Trampas Ridge. This route was traversed with difficulty by those Moragans who needed to transact business in San Ramon. During WW II, the U.S. Army maintained an anti-aircraft installation atop the ridge, and an access road was constructed along the old trail adjacent to the creek through Bollinger Canyon. It was intended that this new road would continue down the east face of Las Trampas Ridge into the San Ramon watershed, linking the two prospective communities: San Ramon and Moraga.

After the war, however, that plan was thwarted by the concerted efforts of environmentalists who did not want to open both of the undeveloped valleys to major new development. The East Bay Regional Park was then established and seized the ridge-top land, which blocked the new road. Thereafter, the east end of the proposed route was abandoned; only a relatively short stretch of the route was later developed as Bollinger Canyon Road into downtown San Ramon. The west end of the blocked route continued to be called Bollinger Canyon Road, which runs from St. Mary's Road through the canyon, and stops at a private ranch on the west face of Las Trampas Ridge.[32]

Blocking the Bollinger Canyon Road was a fortunate outcome for Lamorinda. For those who treasured the open space that otherwise would have been invaded, the development on both sides of Las Trampas Ridge would not have been a pretty picture.

Based on Google MapGIS and Sandy Kimball, Moraga's Pride: Rancho Laguna de los Palos Colorado, *171-2. Annotations by author.*

Shepherd Canyon Freeway

Coinciding with the purchase of the Moraga Company by Utah Construction, the Shepherd Canyon Freeway was planned to connect Oakland (Alameda County) to the Moraga valley (Conta Costa County). The California Highway Commission proposed that this freeway would follow the same route as the SN Railway (OA&E line), but it would require a much larger tunnel under the summit of Oakland Hills. Passing Eastport in Contra Costa County, the route would cross Indian Valley on a nearly straight route south of present-day Miramonte High School and the old Moraga Adobe, where there would be an interchange at Ivy Drive. The route would then cross present-day Moraga Commons, following the present-day Lafayette-Moraga Trail, passing north of St Mary's College, to another interchange at Rohrer Drive in Lafayette. The route would then veer east through the present-day Lafayette Community Park to Burton Drive and another interchange. Then it would push farther east to the vicinity of Glenside Drive and Reliez Station Road, meeting yet another interchange. From there, the route would wind through the hills along present-day Pleasant Hill Road, and connect to Highway 24, which at that time was designated State Route 75 running into Walnut Creek.[33]

The Shepherd Canyon route was designated as Route 77. It was intended to be a four-lane, high-speed freeway through Moraga and Lafayette—the kind that developers of the Moraga Rancho had been dreaming about for years. But the proposal was hotly contested by Utah Construction and a citizens' group called the Orinda-Moraga Homeowners Association.[34] The battle over the freeway raged for several years.[35] Ultimately, the State abandoned the project in 1972, according to CalTrans because of "lack of interest by the county and the cities involved. It was hoped [that] BART might solve the area's traffic snarls."[36]

Gateway Boulevard

Gateway Boulevard was designed to connect the Gateway exit on State Route 24 (then designated State Route 75) to the Moraga Center area via a route passing west of a present-day PG&E switch station (Lost Valley Dr at Don Gabriel Way), and connecting to Shepherd Canyon Freeway in the vicinity of Miramonte High School and the Moraga Adobe. This plan was of great interest to Moragans for more than thirty years: It was designated State Route 93, and would leave Hwy 24 (Route 75) at the Gateway off ramp, follow the old road southeast into the Moraga Valley and past the Moraga Adobe, meeting the Shepherd Canyon Freeway (Route 77) west of the Moraga Center. However, the State dropped the plan when the plans for Shepherd Canyon Freeway were abandoned. The Town of Moraga purchased the surplus State land through which the Gateway route would have traversed, and then leased the land to Moraga Country Club for their 18-hole golf course.[37]

With any future Gateway freeway blocked, and the Shepherd Canyon Freeway abandoned by the State, Moraga then acquired the State land that had been the proposed right of way for the Shepherd Canyon Freeway to traverse the site of the present-day Moraga Commons. The Town of Moraga also purchased significant land along the old SN railway bed past St. Mary's College. These acquisitions further sealed the fate of any freeways passing through Moraga. So much for the Moraga loop. And for all this, Lafayette should be eternally grateful to Moraga.

Incorporation of the Town

As early as 1950, a group of Moraga citizens formed the Moraga Community Association, which attempted to influence the powers in the nearby city of Martinez, the county seat, where county-wide planning policies were formed. Things did not go well for the association; the powers-that-be in Martinez paid little serious attention to the Moraga folks. But, sparked by growing enthusiasm for local control, a cadre of hard-core Moraga volunteers formed. The group consistently objected to the "Martinez mentality," which was pro-growth and threatened many Moragans. The persistent sentiment was that Moragans wanted limited growth.

By 1963, public discussions had begun on incorporation. Based on the concept of an incorporated Moraga under citizen control and with a local government, a committee for incorporation was formed. Not long after, a campaign that featured a speakers' bureau and all the paraphernalia of a vigorous political campaign was launched. The political lines were starkly drawn. Conversely, the anti-incorporation camp included pro-growth advocates who were large landowners and developers, and much of the business community. Those favoring incorporation included all those who did not want Moraga to become a place of high-rise buildings, suburban sprawl, and congestion, and those who objected to Moraga affairs being dictated by a remote county government. The election of November 5, 1974 drew 6,216 voters: 60 percent were in favor of incorporation, 40 percent were opposed. The Town of Moraga was born.[38]

Town officers were selected, and a rudimentary town staff was hired. The first department formed was for planning, and the immediate task was preparation of a General Plan. The 1980 General Plan limited Moraga to 23,000 residents, even though the census that year reported 16,000 residents, 84 percent of whom occupied single-family homes. At about that time, a 169-home housing development was proposed that would cover much of Mulholland Ridge in the center of town. This proposal was subsequently downsized to 110 homes. Even so, the project caused an outrage, and led to a referendum on open-space preservation. The result was the Moraga Open Space Ordinance (MOSO), which prohibited development on ridgelines and severely restricted development density on hillsides. The referendum passed by a slim margin, and lawsuits were launched against the town. In addition to constitutional issues, the complaints against the town pointed out that MOSO implementation had not been thought out carefully. In response, the town imposed a moratorium on new development until MOSO implementation could be sorted out, a process that lasted until 1987.[39]

The struggle between those who championed some growth and those who wanted none endured for years thereafter. Any proposal for development was met with resistance, at times fiercely so. As of 1999, there were nearly 5,800 homes in Moraga, and the impetus of the 2000 General Plan revision was strengthening the open-space protection provisions. This was contentious, pitting major landowners against the Moraga Town Council. Arguments over development potential extended the approval of the new General Plan until 2002.[40]

Then, in 2008, an attempt was made to further strengthen the provisions of MOSO, essentially prohibiting any development in open space on hillsides. This was a countermeasure in response to a ballot measure by a major landowner to permit hillside development. The counter measure was dubbed "Son of MOSO," which was opposed by several groups of voters, not all of whom were major landowners. Both measures were defeated, yet the sentiments were there to see. Most Moragans continued to object to growth that was not carefully planned with an eye toward preservation of Moraga's open space. But it was clear that most voters wanted such regulations to be reasonable and legally defensible.

Over the following several years, further attempts to clarify zoning and design guidelines for hillside development, driven largely by the anti-growth people, resulted in more new rules. The new regulations adopted in 2016 drew legal objections from affected landowners. By no means was new development on open space a settled issue. But gone were the days of the single landowner who did much as he pleased.

Schools

The first school in Moraga was the Willow Springs School, a single-room affair located in a field west of present-day Moraga Commons. A second single-room school called the Moraga School was situated at Glorietta—actually within the Orinda limits. Over the years, the Moraga School attracted more students and Willow Springs suffered from lack of funding and a shortage of qualified teachers. After 1900, the Willow Springs Schoolhouse was replaced with a more substantial building located on present-day School Street, and the teaching staff was stabilized. However, by 1924, the school in Moraga again was experiencing financial difficulties, and the school in Orinda—known still as the Moraga School—agreed to accept children from Moraga. This redefined the Moraga School

District's boundaries, which in effect ceded territory to the Orinda School District. Moraga population projections during the 1960 never materialized, and Moraga closed one of its elementary campuses (Los Perales) in 1967. When Moraga city limits were established after incorporation, the town's boundaries were defined by the school district boundaries. This had the effect of allocating a substantial part of northern Moraga along Moraga Way to become the southern part of Orinda.[41]

The first high school in the Moraga Rancho vicinity was Mt. Diablo High School in Concord. However, Lamorinda growth justified establishing Acalanes High School and the Acalanes Union High School District. The first high school within the rancho was Miramonte High School (1955); the second was Campolindo (1962), located at the original Laguna de los Palos Colorados (known at that time as Tule Lake). Miramonte was located on the Orinda-Moraga city limits, far removed from the major portion of Orinda that was situated north of Highway 24.[42]

The Moraga and Orinda school districts operate as autonomous agencies. All the high schools in the Lamorinda area are part of the Acalanes Union High School District. None of the school districts are related to the governments of Town of Moraga, City of Orinda, or City of Lafayette in any manner other than politically. Whatever cooperation exists among the multiple school agencies and the three cities is based entirely on interpersonal relationships.

Police Services

In the early days, law enforcement in Moraga was the responsibility of the Contra County Sheriff. Given the spread of the sparsely settled rancho, law enforcement was uneven and not a sure thing. When the Town of Moraga was incorporated, Moraga joined with Lafayette and the two cities contracted with the County sheriff for police services. This did not work very well. In the view of many Moragans, Lafayette was receiving a disproportionate share of the contracted sheriff deputies' attention. In the Moraga spirit of local control, Moraga formed a study committee that addressed how best to provide Moraga with its own police force. In 1980, a ten-member Moraga police force was formed, and was comprised of deputies hired from the East Bay Regional Park District and the City of Berkeley; the police chief came from the East Bay Regional Park District. Moraga continued to contract with the sheriff for certain specialized police services, but the force operated as a part of the Town of Moraga and was dedicated entirely to Moraga law enforcement. Lafayette and Orinda continued to contract for their police services directly from the Contra Costa Sheriff, which continues to the present day.[43]

In the years that followed, the Moraga police force grew to thirteen and stabilized. For the past decade, the town has enjoyed a reputation for being one of the safer cities in Contra Costa and the Bay Area. The decision to form an independent police force has been vindicated by comparative peer city expenditures for police services: Moraga's expenditures are less than Lafayette's, and much less than Orinda's.[44]

Fire Protection

In the early days, firefighting capability in Moraga was provided by volunteers. In 1946, the County Board of Supervisors established the first Moraga Fire Department as part of a new fire protection district for West Contra Costa County. The Moraga operation remained all-volunteer, but given the enormous geographical extent of the new county district, Moraga received very little attention. In 1950, Moraga had 200 residents and 45 homes, so the arrangement was barely acceptable. As the community grew, however, things had to change. By 1955, the town had acquired a single fire truck and a 3-man paid staff of firefighters, plus some 25 volunteers stationed at a building in the Moraga Ranch compound. By 1968, Moraga had created its own Moraga Fire Protection District, and had built a new fire station on Moraga Way.[45]

Moraga's isolated location caused concern for medical emergencies. Another volunteer organization called Rescue One created a foundation to fund emergency medical response facilities, including a fully stocked ambulance. The firefighting crew became dual-trained as emergency medical technicians (EMT). Moraga now had its own emergency medical response capability, entirely separate from the County's emergency medical services.[46]

The Moraga EMT/paramedic capability caught the eye of Orindans who shared Moraga's concern for inadequate county response to medical emergencies on the remote western end of the county. The Moraga and Orinda city councils formed a joint study committee, which addressed the concept of a new district for fire protection and emergency medical services serving Moraga, Orinda, and Canyon. A plan for a consolidated district was approved by 80 percent of voters of Moraga and Orinda in 1997. Thereafter, an additional fire station was constructed in Moraga across Moraga Road from the Rheem Center, and old and obsolete stations were replaced in Orinda. The new district, called MOFD, remains responsible for serving Moraga and Orinda, plus Canyon and the unincorporated areas around Moraga.[47]

MOFD has its own governing board with representatives from five districts within Moraga and Orinda. The MOFD board reports to neither the Moraga nor Orinda councils. MOFD board members are directly elected by the voters in the districts they represent, but the relationships between the district and the cities are entirely interpersonal. MOFD continues to deliver exceptional fire protection services to this day.

However, the Contra Costa Fire Protection District has repeatedly attempted to have MOFD dissolved, and all MOFD revenues and assets turned over to the county. This has drawn rapid and strong objection from Moraga in particular, and to a lesser extent by Orinda. It's no secret that the firefighter's union is behind these takeover maneuvers, and it is expected that the union will launch new attempts to install their preferred candidates every time a board vacancy occurs. These episodes have caused vigorous reactions in the past, and no doubt will again in the future. So far, neither the Moraga nor Orinda city councils appear to be at all interested in tearing down something that works so well for the local communities that MOFD was created to serve.

Parks and Recreation

That Moraga places emphasis on its parks and the recreational opportunities available to its citizens and anyone visiting, is reflected in the town's history and its current General Plan. The earliest development planning by the land barons included some grandiose plans for parks, and as the Town of Moraga came into being, many plans of the past began to take shape.

The Christian Brothers at St. Mary's used the Hacienda property from 1961, when Donald Rheem turned the property over to the order. The Hacienda served as the Christian Brothers' headquarters for over ten years until 1973, when the property was sold to the Moraga Park and Recreation Authority. After incorporation, the Town of Moraga named the property "Hacienda de las Flores" intending it be a public park, a place for holding classes, social events and public meetings, and for use as town offices.[48] Much of the land on the original Rheem estate was subdivided, and homes were built surrounding the Hacienda building and its grounds. The Hacienda property was used as intended for the next thirty years, until changes were made (see details in Chapter 7).

When the state declared the land that would have been occupied by the Shepherd Canyon Freeway as surplus, the Town of Moraga jumped at the opportunity to acquire it. This 20-acre parcel became the Moraga Commons. Largely through the efforts of volunteer service groups, the town created features that made Moraga Commons a public park offering a wide range of recreational amenities. Not only Moragans benefited from this new park; many visitors from nearby communities have enjoyed the place over the years.[49]

At about the same time, the town acquired an 8.5-acre parcel on the southeast end of the town; the parcel became Rancho Laguna Park. Intended for use as a passive park, largely for nature appreciation, this small appendage to the town instead became the focus of some bitter disputes among citizens around 2010.

In 2016, the town was granted 2.53 acres of vacant land west of Moraga Road and opposite the Moraga Commons. The land was residual acreage from a small subdivision within the Moraga Specific Plan Area farther to the west (see details in Chapter 6). In 2012, the land was dedicated as a passive park after minor improvements were made, including pathways and a foot bridge providing access to the park.

Moragans have jealously guarded their parks and recreation program since at least the 1960s. However, in 2003, a miscue in Moraga governance upset things. An interim town manager had been hired while the search for a permanent town manager could be completed. At the time, the town's budget was strained by unexpected expenses and disappointing revenues. When looking for ways to trim expenses, the interim manager zeroed in on the park and recreation department. Reasoning that economies of scale could be realized, the interim manager arranged a deal with Lafayette to have Lafayette take over Moraga's recreation department functions, which included all of the town's recreation programs. Revenues would be split between Lafayette and Moraga. However, Moraga got the short end of the deal, and Moragans weren't happy. No doubt memories of the early unhappy experiences with the joint police services and unsatisfactory services of countywide fire protection stoked suspicions that a bad deal had been made. When the permanent town manager was installed, he immediately hired a new parks and recreation director who terminated the arrangement with Lafayette. Whatever possessed the Town Council at the time to authorize the deal has never been entirely explained. It was sad to hear people rejoice that Moraga had "taken back recreation from Lafayette."[50]

What this Moraga history demonstrates is that those who call Moraga home are a determined and independent lot. The early arrivals came to a sparsely settled and remote land where their solitude was guaranteed by the remoteness of the vast Moraga Rancho. That's the way they liked it, and that's what they sought to preserve in the years that followed.

Over the following decades, land barons hardly changed that mindset, and neither did the squatters and lumberjacks and ranchers who came to settle in the rancho. The railroad opened the rancho to the outside world, but the attitudes of those who lived there did not change much. Moragans wanted to control their own lives without interference from outside. And as the rancho lands were developed—slowly over the long haul but in spurts after World War II—struggles over local control became serious as competing interests of landowners and developers clashed with lovers of the semi-rural environment who had escaped the cities for a better way of life. Politics became intensely local. What mattered first and foremost were the self-interests on either side of any argument. This notably came to a head in 1974, when a majority of Moragans seized control and won incorporation. But they didn't stop there. They went on to create their own independent police department, and then a fire department. It was all about preserving their preferred lifestyles and retaining local control. It remains so to this day.

CHAPTER 4

What's Important

MORAGA'S HISTORY—a period spanning about 150 years—has been shaped by the character of the people who live there. For most of that time, the land that became Moraga was under the control of only a few landowners. First were the original Mexican homesteaders, followed by the land barons, and then the major land developers. Not many people lived in the area that was known as the Moraga Rancho, and the rancho was sparsely settled. Those who arrived then were largely independent, and self-reliance was essential for them to succeed on the land.

But that all began to change when the rancho became recognized as a desirable place to settle. Once the railroad penetrated the area and offered passenger and freight services with cities to the west, changes came to Moraga and neighboring communities. Newcomers began to flow into the rancho. Slowly at first, the population swelled and, after the 1940s, the challenges of increased numbers of newcomers accelerated. Railroad services and the vehicular roadways opened the Moraga Rancho. Moraga was no more an isolated countryside close to, but removed from, the metropolis of Oakland and San Francsico. And the town became faced with urban challenges many Moragans never imagined.

How did they respond? They took matters into their own hands. In remarkably quick time, they mobilized their political energies and won incorporation as an independent city that we know today as the Town of Moraga. Certainly, the new town was a part of Contra Costa County, but it intentionally governed itself and was largely free to regulate the affairs of its citizens according to how they wanted to be governed.

But who were these newcomers? What attitudes did they bring with them? How did they want to live in their new home in Moraga? What were their values and aspirations? How did they blend in with the old-timers who had been Moragans for several generations? And how did everyone respond to the changes imposed on their lives?

Modern-Day Moragans

Those who came to Moraga after the war years tended to do so because of employment in the San Francisco Bay Area. Moraga was a lovely place to raise a family, which had been the message promoters like Robert Barnes of the Moraga Company shouted since the early 1900s. Developers like Russell Bruzzone took great pleasure in providing these new families with their own homes. Thus, the town grew rapidly as one subdivision after another was completed. By the early 1970s, some 5,800 homes were occupied, about 85 percent as single-family dwellings. The population reached about 14,500 persons. By 2020 the population reached 16,868 and has since decreased slightly. Total population doesn't vary much year on year.

The newcomers were largely homogeneous; they were not particularly diverse in ethnic terms. They tended to be an educated lot, many with advanced degrees. They were largely professionals, and they were almost all relatively well-off economically. They came from all over the country, many from East Coast cities, rarely as refugees from depressed parts of the country. They came to live and prosper in Moraga and remain there. Aging in place was presumed.

Most newcomers came for the rural ambience. They referred to Moraga as "semi-rural." They cherished the open spaces of the town and its surrounding lands, and they enjoyed communing with nature, which was right before them in the urban-wildland interface beyond the town limits.

They also came for the schools, which had acquired enviable reputations for excellence at all levels. Academic achievements of Moraga students were evident in the high levels of matriculation to prestigious colleges and universities all over the country. School athletics and programs in the arts were widely recognized as exceptional. St. Mary's College was among the best small colleges in the country, of which Moragans were proud. Some young Moragans spent their undergraduate years at the college, and the college's post-graduate professional degree programs were popular for numerous Moragans.

Many newcomers came with strong religious convictions of all faiths. The town's many places of worship provided sanctuary and broad opportunities for civic involvement at all age levels. Church life was important, although not dominant, for many.

Many came with strong senses of community commitment. This translated into volunteerism, and the many service clubs and organizations within the town made contributing time and treasure natural for many Moragans. Numerous wonderful things that happened in town were the fruits of volunteer contributions. Newcomers were invited to join these efforts, and many did so gladly.

Volunteerism extended to public service in Moraga government. While small in physical size, the town was complex in its organization. Numerous boards, commissions, and committees were populated by volunteers who thought nothing of donating their time to the town and their fellow citizens. From the early days, it's what made the place work.

Self-Determination

Early Moragans did not like to be told what they could and could not do. They cherished their independence and resented being instructed by anyone, let alone someone from afar. They wanted to do things, and decide things, for themselves. They were not inclined to ask for help; no doubt they recognized that help from others was likely to entail something in return at some later time. Self-determination came to be the defining characteristic of these people.

Things didn't change much in the years that followed. The newcomers were attracted to the freedom of the place, and that's how they wanted it to remain. They much preferred having control over their own lives. To the extent possible, they wanted—and still do—to determine their own futures.

Intrinsic Values

The values held dear by Moragans, the fundamental concepts that underlie how they live as citizens of the town, are, to this day, expressed in two ways: formally in their town's constitution, and informally in the ways that they act.

According to the General Plan:

> Moragans' core values are the basis for how they plan and run their community. California State Law requires every incorporated city to have and maintain a General Plan, which essentially is the constitution for the city. The first part of the plan is a concise statement of core values and guiding principles that serve as overarching goals of the General Plan. The values statement reflects the character of the citizens of the town. Every policy the city makes, and every regulation that is adopted, must conform to the core values as stated in their General Plan.[1]

The 2002 General Plan enumerates the town's core values. Moraga citizens value:[2]

- **Environmental Preservation:** The town's natural setting, open space, environmental resources, and natural recreation opportunities.

- **Community Design and Character:** The town's semi-rural setting, its well-maintained homes, abundant landscaping, and high design standards; the sense of community and opportunities to get together, formally and informally.

- **Mobility:** The ability to move to and from other communities with relative ease; having free and convenient parking within town; being able to move easily about town, including by bicycle and by walking; freedom to use available technologies to allow working from home; and allowing in-home offices.

- **Shopping and Services:** The importance of the local business community for their shopping and service offerings, and for their civic and community involvement.

- **Housing:** Quality housing options that allow children, seniors, and the local workforce to continually call Moraga home.

- **Community Facilities:** Excellent schools, parks, library, youth activities, senior services, and recreational opportunities; St. Mary's College as a part of the community, and healthy working relationships with college administrators, faculty, and students.

- **Public Safety:** Living in a safe environment.

- **Community Decision-Making:** Citizen activism and volunteerism, and citizens having a voice in decision-making; working relations with neighboring cities and regional agencies; and working relationships with landowners and developers.

Values Observed in Political Discourse

Beyond the core values statement in the General Plan, several values are evident from the town's political affairs:[3]

Freedom of Expression

Moragans take their constitutionally guaranteed rights to free expression seriously. Whatever the forum, one can count on Moragans to say (or write) what they want, on nearly any subject. This is healthy, but it also carries some risks. While one is entirely free to say what one wants, one is also free to make a fool of oneself. Modern-day social media heighten this risk since anyone can broadcast their uncensored opinions as widely as they wish, perhaps more widely than they intend. While it's laudable that people are free to express themselves, it's often lamentable that, at times, some do so unwisely and, perhaps, carelessly or recklessly. It's not that they intend this outcome; sometimes they just can't help themselves.

Property rights

Most citizens value the property rights of other citizens: What's mine is mine, what's yours is yours. However, such isn't always the case: What's yours is oftentimes open for discussion. Tensions sometimes are evident when a private property owner wants to do something with his property, but some individual or group of citizens are opposed. If the property owner's proposal entirely conforms to existing town regulations, there really is no basis for opposing it. But what sometimes happens is that opposition becomes so vehement that the property owner loses the argument, and his property rights are violated. Once a matter becomes deeply political, emotions can overwhelm everything else. It's not unusual for the opposition to win.

Children first and foremost

The value some people assign to the well-being of their children sometimes trumps anything else. When it comes to schools, nothing else seems important. Such primacy, when taken to extremes, can block commonsense decisions on allocation of scarce resources, like tax dollars or use of property of either schools or the town. Balanced perspective is appropriate, but this isn't always the case.

Safety for self and family

Safety of one's own person and property, and for that of the person's family, often trumps the safety of the wider community. There are times when a broader community view is better than satisfying the needs of special interests. But occasionally this value isn't shared by everyone. The tensions thereby created become particularly evident around the broad matter of traffic safety. A surprising number of citizens refuse to acknowledge that supporting initiatives to improve traffic safety are preferred over catering to their own narrow interests.

Enjoyment of life

It is clear that, as a whole, Moragans cherish their recreational opportunities, and eagerly support community activities aimed at wider enjoyment. Nonetheless, there are those who will not tolerate community activities that they feel invade the private enjoyment of their own lives. This becomes an issue when a community activity (such as a band concert) generates bothersome noise. This situation occurs annually when the summer concert series engages performing groups who crank up the sound, which inevitably draws complaints from aggrieved neighbors. Mitigation measures in some situations are never enough, and community activities are often curtailed. The community thereby suffers.

Civility

Getting along with others is something most Moragans expect, especially in civic discourse. Nothing is less productive than a petitioner insulting someone else in the public arena. Nothing draws more criticism than public officials waging a verbal attack on a colleague. Civility is expected. Civility is demanded. Bad manners are not condoned.

Expectation for Local Government

From the early days of post-1960s, it was evident that Moragans wanted minimum local government. While some people preferred hardly any government at all, most accepted that minimum services government could be achieved. In the early days, this was a stated goal. But what that philosophy entailed was constraining the town government from doing much, if anything. Budget restrictions were always an impediment to getting anything done. In many instances, constraints on staff in terms of their numbers and their qualifications led to some departments being incapable of doing what needed to be done. This was fine for many Moragans—it was the low-cost way to go—but it meant gradual deterioration of the town's properties and the services provided to the citizens. It was going to require a lot of effort to change this self-defeating mindset.

Yet, many Moragans, particularly newcomers, expected town government to deliver the things they wanted. Some newcomers expected things that were commensurate with what they had experienced in the places they'd left, where those local governments were staffed and funded to accomplish a lot (not that they actually did). These new Moragans expected that the town had the resources and the will to make things happen. However, many of them didn't want to pay for anything, and they objected when they were told they might have to. Aspirations thwarted by public paucity set the tone for many years of agonizing effort on the part of town staff and those who volunteered to help make things happen.

Attitudes Toward Change

Perhaps the greatest challenge for anyone trying to achieve anything was the mindset of many Moragans, both the old-timers and those who had arrived recently, that not much needed to be done. Several dimensions of the Moraga mindset presented challenges.

First was the attitude that "if it ain't broke, don't fix it." This was plain to see in the condition of the town's aging infrastructure: roads, bridges, storm drainage, and buildings.

Deferred maintenance was business as usual. After all, if deterioration is gradual, it is sometimes hardly noticed.

Second was the view that the town couldn't spend money it didn't have. "We can't afford it!" was the lament so often heard. What was rare was any discussion about finding ways to raise the funds that would support doing things that needed to be done. A more common discussion revolved around finding cheaper ways to do things, which predictably led to some shoddy results. This was especially evident with road maintenance.

A third impediment was the often-heard saying that "process is our most important product." This was particularly evident in the town's onerous development regulations, which required that developers do some things seen in no other city in the area. The complexity of Moraga's regulatory apparatus has served a useful purpose, in the minds of those inclined to curtail new development. It has slowed things to a crawl, in some instances discouraging project proponents from proceeding with their proposals, or warning others not to even try. The result has been under-investment in the town. This became particularly evident in the condition of the town's shopping centers.

A fourth feature of the mindset was throttling the town's ability to perform: Some town departments were woefully undersized given their mandates; some were staffed by individuals who had no qualifications other than, perhaps, friendships with other staff.

But the most serious issue of the Moraga mindset was low expectations. As a plaque mounted in the local hardware store says, "On this site in 1897 nothing happened." While the plaque provokes a smile for some, it is cynical. The town seemed stagnated and going nowhere, and it remained to be seen whether this could be changed.[4]

Bronze plaque mounted at Moraga Hardware & Lumber, 2023. Courtesy of Bill Snider, proprietor. (Photo by author).

CHAPTER 5

Difficult People

MORAGA TOWN GOVERNMENT is made up of citizens and a small group of hired professionals. Together they comprise a variety of people with widely diverse talents and temperaments. For anything to be accomplished, those within the town government must get along with one another, and they must have the support of the citizenry. Otherwise, very little can be accomplished. None of this is an easy matter.

Form of Government

Like many of the incorporated cities of California, Moraga operates with a council-manager form of government.[1] The "council" comprises five directly elected voters of the town, who serve four-year terms. The "manager" is a hired professional in the business of running a city (the town). The town manager reports to the Town Council and is responsible for all town operations. The manager supervises the daily activities of departments, with notable exceptions in Moraga of fire protection, schools, library services, water supply, sewage, and telecommunications. For those functions, separate agencies are involved, and the manager is expected to build and maintain working relationships with the agencies that provide those services.[2]

A healthy relationship between a town manager and Town Council is essential. A manager without council support is dead in the water; a council without the respect of the manager can become frustrated as the manager might seem out of control. Council directions can be misunderstood, ignored, or (worse) disobeyed. Sometimes the manager-council relationship becomes poisonous and outright hostile. Manager insubordination can become serious. If effective counseling cannot correct the relationship, the council had best rid itself of the manager and hire someone who can work agreeably in the relationship.

Sometimes a manager considers his/her relationship with a council as coequals. It is not. Town Councils such as in Moraga have five members; there is no sixth council member. It's amazing that sometimes a heady manager doesn't recognize this fundamental employer-employee relationship. Insubordination cannot be tolerated.[3]

The town manager is usually responsible for recruiting, hiring, and retaining suitable staff to carry out each department's responsibilities. The council's part in any of this should be tolerated only to the extent that the manager invites council participation. If staff performance is not corrected by the manager, the council should think twice before renewing the manager's employment contract.

As a matter of policy, Moraga operates essentially as "a contract services town when it is cost-effective, contracting out all work that is beyond the capability of town staff."[4] Town staff is leveraged with professional services consultancies who are contracted for specific purposes. Sometimes a consultant is retained for an extended period of service, but most of the time the scope of services is project-oriented with a defined start and completion, and a control budget. Consultants report to their respective staff departments or to the town manager. The Town Council has no part in the staff-consultant relationship other than approving engagement contracts and approving payment claims.

A special consultant is the town attorney. Moraga is fortunate to have had the same town attorney for several decades. Some cities religiously change attorneys in an apparent attempt to "keep legal counsel on its toes." In Moraga's case, this has never been necessary. Moraga's longtime town attorney diligently attends to management of legal matters and helps safeguard town officials from straying into legal minefields. Moreover, the value of institutional knowledge justifies retaining the same attorney over the long haul. It works well. So Moraga Town Council has not tried to fix what's not broken.

Citizen Involvement and Volunteerism

Moraga's long tradition of citizen involvement is institutionalized as a stated goal in the town's General Plan: ". . . [Involvement] of citizens as human resources to research problems and recommend solutions."[5] Moreover, it's a town policy to "[solicit] and utilize citizen expertise in non-paid committee and special service functions, using citizens committees as an extension of staff whenever possible. Strive for broad numbers in terms of numbers and diversity."[6] This practice has served the town well in the past, and it will surely pay dividends in the future.

In past years, there was rarely a problem recruiting volunteers to join an effort to get something done. People customarily have been willing to lend themselves unselfishly to causes they consider worthy of joining. They do so enthusiastically. Enlightened leaders of commissions, committees, or task forces demonstrate their leadership competence by identifying and recruiting effective volunteers. Such leaders are more likely to produce good results.

However, in recent years, recruiting volunteers has met some unexpected resistance. Not all newcomers are inclined to contribute nearly as freely as have others in past years. Why is this? Perhaps competing pressures of their professions or restrictions due to family obligations. Sometimes it's simply cultural: Not all newcomers come from traditions where volunteerism is valued. Nonetheless, it's important that citizens realize that many of the things that happen in a small town like Moraga do so because volunteers make them happen. It isn't always acceptable to take the view that "Someone else can do it." Perhaps it would be better if those folks ask themselves, "Why can't I do this?" . . . then join in an effort to do it.

It's not uncommon nowadays that newcomers are issue-driven, especially where the issues are national in character and tend to conform to national-level politics. However, this can change quickly when local issues emerge and gain prominence, often when someone's self-interests are threatened and the local issues take on lives of their own. Indeed, some local issues can dominate people's thinking, shaping their views on all sorts of other matters. These people tend to volunteer where their self-interest lies. If there's a threat that they think they should counter, they are apt to join in an effort to serve their own interest. After all . . . All Politics Is Local!

Individuals and the Public Process

Moragans continually demonstrate their fondness for public process. They want to know what's happening, and they generally want to be part of it. They like the freedom to express themselves, make their opinions known, and offer their suggestions. Indeed, a lot of citizens demand such participation, and they can become agitated when denied it. But though they want opportunities to be involved, they can become angry when it becomes inconvenient, or impossible, for them to do so. It's a never-ending challenge for the Town Council, mayor, and town staff to ensure that no barriers interfere with citizen participation.

What some citizens fail to appreciate, however, is that active participation requires some work on their part. Citizens must be vigilant and aware of what's happening; they must seek out information and do their homework. No one will spoon-feed them. The town can make information available through various media, but citizens must pick up the information and study it. Everything recorded in the course of public business is open to public scrutiny, but it requires commitment on the citizen's part.

All too frequently, some citizens perform in public in ways that demonstrate contempt. It's not uncommon for a citizen with a bone to pick to hurl insults at the Town Council or at the town staff. Sometimes these attacks are ad hominem. Rarely are they productive.

Never are they justified. If something can't be said civilly, it should not be said, at least in a public forum. Town staff are hired to do their jobs, which do not include being denigrated publicly. Most elected officials accept the inevitability that such attacks will someday happen. That's what they signed up for, so they're obliged to manage the attacks in civil ways. This can be challenging when dealing with especially difficult people.

Behaviors: Good and Bad

Anyone's public behavior is a manifestation of the person's personality and the circumstances of the moment. Dealing with those who are not performing at their best requires some skills that many people don't have. These are skills that I am constantly trying to develop. Over the course of eighteen years in town government, I found myself in plenty of situations dealing with some truly difficult people. As an official in local government, there is no option: "You can choose your friends, but you can't choose your voters." So one must figure out how best to manage difficult people, and how to manage oneself.

Fortunately, there are some effective training programs available to public officials that can help.[7] In their bestselling motivational book, *Dealing with People You Can't Stand*, naturopathic physicians, speakers, and trainers on "The Art of Change," Drs. Rick Brinkman and Rick Kirschner introduce their subject of dealing with difficult people with the following framing:

> People you can't stand: they're those difficult people who are either not doing things you want them to do or doing things you do not want them to do—and you don't know what to do about them. . . . [W]hile you can't change these people, you can find ways to communicate with them. . . . It's a matter of knowing how to get through to them while they are behaving badly.[8]

Brinkman and Kirschner (I refer to them as the "counselors") suggest ten specific patterns of behavior that sane people resort to when they feel threatened or thwarted. These patterns are worth learning because, during my experiences in the public arena, I've observed them all and have been obliged to deal with all these problematic people. The counselors refer to them in terms of their "10 Most Unwanted List." (See chart.)[9]

Brinkman & Kirschner's
10 Most Unwanted List

The Tank   Confrontational, pointed, and angry, the ultimate in pushy and aggressive behavior.

The Sniper   Whether through rude comments, biting sarcasm, or well-honed rolls of the eyes, making you look foolish.

The Grenade   After a brief period of calm, the grenade explodes into unfocused ranting and raving about things that have nothing to do with the present circumstances.

The Know-It-All   Seldom in doubt, has a low tolerance for correction or contradiction. If something goes wrong, will speak with the same authority about who is to blame—you!

The Think-They-Know-It-All   Can't fool all of the people all of the time but can fool some of the people enough of the time, and enough of the people all of the time—all for the sake of getting some attention.

The Yes Person   In an effort to please people and avoid confrontation, says yes without thinking things through; usually forgets other commitments, overcommits, and ends up feeling resentful.

The Maybe Person   In a moment of decision, procrastinates in the hope that a better choice will present itself.

The Nothing Person   No verbal feedback, no nonverbal feedback. Nothing.

The No Person   Disguised as a mild-mannered normal person, fights a never-ending battle for futility, hopelessness, and despair.

The Whiner   Feels helpless and overwhelmed by an unfair world; a perfectionist, and no one and nothing measures up to their standards; try and engage you with their problems, which is usually never helpful.

What to do when confronted with such difficult people? One can stay and do nothing, or simply leave the encounter. Sometimes these options work since they allow some cooling-off time. But these are merely expedient solutions; the difficult person is likely to perform similarly at some future time.

Then there's the option of changing one's attitude toward the difficult person. But first, you must try and understand the focus and intent of the other person. Are they striving for control or seeking attention? Are they hoping for perfection in the task at hand, or just looking for approval?

Then there's the option of changing one's own behavior. To this end, the counselors offer this suggestion:

> The behavior of the people you can't stand is determined by their perceptions of what they think is going on as it relates to what they think is important. Their behavior interacts with your behavior, which is based on your perception of these same variables. The results of your dealings with people at their worst is, in large measure, up to you.[10]

The counselors suggest "people want to be heard and understood." The intent that any serious person brings to communication is usually positive. Things may go awry, but that was not their original intent. So, the challenge is to figure out what the difficult person's positive intent was before things went sideways. This requires patience, listening skills, and tolerance. It also depends in large measure on the tone of your voice and the body language that expresses how you feel about the other person. "Honesty can be effective no matter what difficult behavior people engage in if you tell your truth in a way that builds them up rather than tears them down. The more trust you have with people, the more likely it is you will be heard."[11] It's essential to convince the difficult person that they are valued, that their contribution is important, and that they will be heard. It's not important to agree with the person; just understand them. As the counselors suggest, assume the best and "give the benefit of the doubt."[12]

The counselors further suggest some pithy ideas for changing one's own attitude when dealing with a difficult person. They frame their suggestions as ways one might talk to oneself:[13]

> "The branch that bends with the snow lives to see another winter, but the branch that resists the snow breaks. . . . When you resist, it's usually you who breaks, not the difficult person."

> "Somewhere in this experience is an opportunity."

"Any experience I can learn from is a good one."

"I can be flexible."

"I know that anything is possible. . . . The people who believe that anything is possible are the ones who get the breakthroughs."

"Oh well. . . . Let it go, and go on from there."

"All things must pass. . . . Think for a moment how old you are and about all you've been through. . . . If you look into the future with that knowledge, you may gain perspective and make the whole process easier on yourself."

"This used to bother me. That's all behind me now. . . . Why not start talking about your reaction to the difficult person as if the situation is already behind you?"

"In God we trust. . . . Hang in there. Or let go. In due season, everything will be revealed and resolved."

These morsels of advice seem to work . . . for me, at least. I found myself being able to endure some unpleasant encounters without serious damage. The counselors' advice rings of a similar thought offered by Tip O'Neill:

"Keep your perspective. . . . Take your job seriously but don't take yourself seriously."[14]

Learning to Deal with Them

Following are some of the thoughts on suggestions the counselors offer on how to deal with difficult people. Their advice has helped me personally.

The Tank

When under attack by the Tank, aggressive behavior is designed to put you back on The Tank's intended course or eliminate you as his obstacle. It's all about control. Because The Tank doesn't attack people he respects, it's necessary to command it. Hold your ground, interrupt the attack, backtrack to The Tank's main point, but think twice before returning fire. If the Tank is right and you're not, admit it. An appropriate *mea culpa* can go a long way.[15]

The Sniper

Looking for control and/or attention. "If you don't like to be teased and sniping wounds you, it may become common knowledge that you're an easy target. Once word gets out, a time will come when someone will try to take advantage of your weakness. . . . And every time you react to the sniping, you'll be setting yourself up, as [The Sniper gains] encouragement to dish out more of the same." So, bring the Sniper out of hiding; publicly acknowledge the person, question the Sniper's intent and relevancy to the issue. It's possible to return the sniping, ignore it, or go on a frontal Tank-like attack. But, if the Sniper has a good point, admit it.[16]

Snipers are everywhere. Sometimes they can be a colleague, such as a Town Council member. There was a young council member who had a quick temper during my time on the Town Council; she who wore her credentials on her sleeve. Another council member— the Sniper—was ideologically opposed to the feisty council member, and quickly identified the buttons to push. And that's what the Sniper did, over and over. It was like witnessing torture seeing the feisty council member take the bait time after time, and then feeling terrible reacting when the Sniper hit the right buttons. It was counterproductive. Only after a lot of private counseling of the feisty council member did she realize that she was setting herself up for the Sniper's entertainment.

The Grenade

When people feel their need for attention is thwarted, they can become the Grenade. Their behavior is explosive and unpredictable, sometimes becoming a temper tantrum. They might hate themselves for blowing off. It's usually best to look at the tantrum as something childish, or to look at it as an opportunity for a funny reaction (like a cream pie in the Grenade's face). The important thing is not to react to it; take a break and let things calm down. Most important, find out what pulls the Grenade's pin, and be sure to avoid it in the future.[17]

I witnessed this behavior emerge frequently with a particular citizen (the Grenade), who resented nearly anything the town tried to do. It didn't take much for the Grenade to explode, and the spectacle of a grown man ranting in public was not pretty. With all these outbursts, it was best simply to allow the Grenade to make a fool of himself, perhaps realizing afterward that he had left a lousy impression on those who had seen his performance.

The Know-It-All

This person is looking to control. Strive to open the Know-It-All's mind to alternative ideas, but be prepared and know what you're talking about. Try to enlist support and/or participation in pursuing your idea.[18]

Know-It-Alls appeared often when the town's finances were being discussed. They seemed to know what they were talking about, but their knowledge was often shallow. They became defensive when it was pointed out that they might not have entirely understood something. Trying to enlist their support was a nobler idea, but it was not uncommon for the Know-It-All to refuse to become involved: "I've got too much else going on in my life."

The Yes Person
This person is looking for approval by getting along. These are usually nice people, hoping they can be helpful, but they lose sight of what else they have on their plate, or may not realize what's achievable. Make it safe for them to be honest, be honest with them, help them plan, get commitment, and strengthen the relationship.[19]

The Yes Person sometimes appears as a member of a town staff. If assigned to participate in a study group that involves citizens and elected officials, the Yes Person can demonstrate their inability to resist taking on things on which they can't deliver. The Yes Person may be otherwise competent, but in terms of personal management of their own affairs, the Yes Person may be dangerously deficient.

The Think-They-Know-It-All
These people have the ability to learn just enough about something to engage in a conversation and seem to know what they are talking about. They are apt to be addicted to exaggeration and are attention-seeking. They often get defensive when challenged. The problem is, they can sound convincing and can sway other people. So, it's best to let them have their say, and then clarify their points, emphasizing the facts that demonstrate they are wrong. Give them a break, but don't let them do it again.[20]

The Think-They-Know-It-All often makes an appearance when a complex issue is being publicly discussed. This happened when the town was studying potential alternative uses for the Hacienda de las Flores property. A consultant had presented an imaginative report on alternative uses, and the Think-They-Know-It-All rebutted the consultant's recommendations. The rebuttal didn't offer much new information; but it
was damaging. (This issue is explained later in greater depth.)

The Maybe Person
Also an approval seeker, the Maybe Person procrastinates, wobbles, can't decide. Pushing them does no good, so it's best to be kind and help them decide on the thing at hand. Make them comfortable, find out what's bothering them. If this is unclear, show them a decision-making process, reassure them, and follow through.[21]

If the town manager is a Maybe Person, decisions might not be made without a lot of urging by the Town Council. Sometimes, decisions can be coaxed from the manager. If the behavior becomes the norm, perhaps it's time for the manager to work elsewhere.

The Nothing Person

These can be passive people, yet they are usually task-focused. They want to get along but tend toward perfection. They need to get it right for fear of failing; they pull back and refuse to do anything. Patience is essential. Recognize how the person might decide, and help them see how the future could be brighter with decisions.

The Nothing Person appears to be a "diddler." Staff members who behave in this manner are high maintenance; they require a lot of attention. Council members who behave in this manner should ask themselves why they are on the council at all.

The No Person

They are task-focused, motivated by intent to get it right by avoiding mistakes. Often, they are perfectionists. It's crucial to refrain from regarding these people with contempt, so move from problem- and fault-finding toward solutions. It's unlikely they can be convinced things aren't so bad, but it's important to acknowledge their good intent and consider admitting your own fault (assuming there is some culpability). In any event, enlist their help in a new approach, making them a part of change.

The No Person's persistent negativity is draining and can become demoralizing. They can poison a town staff with their constant refusal to go along with anything. They are the town manager's worse nightmare.

The Whiner

The Whiner is intent on getting it right, and compelled by desire for perfection, they are usually passive and become despondent when they believe they have been thwarted. They know things need to change but have no clue about how. Their negativity can infect an organization. They tend to generalize. Don't agree with them but do let them know you want to help make things better, working with them. Listen carefully, get specific, focus on solutions, not problems. Show them a better future.

The Whiner appears in public when offering their comments on an issue, or simply when they are contributing to general public comment. They have a lot to say, but nothing of value to offer. I found them especially insufferable when they returned time and again to whine about the same thing, or to introduce a new thing that distressed them. Most of the time it's best simply to hear them out and thank them for their contributions.

And What If They Can't Stand You?

The challenges of difficult people cut both ways. Indeed, my own behavior is sometimes annoying to others, and sometimes counterproductive. What to do about it? The counselors offer some suggestions to consider:

- Be positive. Consider what's possible rather than focusing on what isn't. Often negativity is self-fulfilling. The Pygmalion effect is real.

- Be honest. Admit you're wrong when it's clear you are. You always look better to others when you do. There's no disgrace in an admission of a mistake.

- Acknowledge any difficult person's intent. Show appreciation for reasonable criticisms.

- Don't let cheap shots land. Throw them back at someone like The Sniper.

- Enlist support of those who criticize, and perhaps enlist their help in doing things differently in the future.

- Focus on solutions, not problem identification, or finding fault. People who are doers waste little time reacting to things. Instead, they use their energy to move in the direction of the possible.

With that body of counsel, Chapter 6 now focuses on getting things done in Moraga.

CHAPTER 6

Things That Got Done

IN MANY PEOPLES' MINDS, Moraga is a place with abundant promise. However, the things that should be done and how rapidly they ought to be done is always open for discussion. When I first joined the town as a planning commissioner, I was impressed by the richness of possibilities for new things and improvements to old ones. But that was just me. Others had their own ideas, and many of the others were prepared to fight to get their way. What I quickly realized was that it was essential to come to agreement on what was truly important, and then figure out how to do the things that were really needed. What I wanted wasn't necessarily what others had in mind. And I had "come to the table" with no idea how difficult and time-consuming it was going to be to garner support for any idea.

And yet, in time, my tenure as a Moraga Planning Commissioner (1999-2004) and as Town Council member (2004-2016) became arguably successful. My visions were met, and a substantial part of the body politic evidently agreed that they were worthwhile. They are still in place. They have survived the test of time.

Following are case studies of the things that went well. Each issue is framed by way of its rough contours. How each issue conformed to public values is identified, as well as the importance that the public attached to it. Citizen involvement is specified, and the course of action that was taken is outlined. The success of each matter is assessed—but how did we know?

Downtown Specific Plan: Goals and Plans

During the lengthy 2002 General Plan process described in Chapter 3, the concept of a specific plan had been introduced. In 2010, the town adopted a specific plan for the Moraga Center area that pursued a vision of a revitalized town center with new housing, offices, shopping, dining, and recreational opportunities.[1] It made sense to everyone on the steering committee, except the major landowner, who owned most of the land within the 187-acre Moraga Center area.

It took eight years of tough negotiation to give birth to the Moraga Center Specific Plan (MCSP) that had been directed in 2002. Once the plan had been adopted, the matter went dormant. The Town Council at that time did not seem to have any interest in pursuing it. The scion of the major landowner family (Russell Bruzzone) had died in 2001, and the family was not interested in doing anything in cooperation with the town toward MCSP implementation. That situation did not change until 2008, when two new Town Council members (Dave Trotter and I) encouraged the town manager and staff to pick up the pace and get something done.

At that time, the town was blessed with an excellent planning director. She began the long process of putting some flesh on the bare bones of the MCSP. The first product was a diagram that showed key opportunities and a possible configuration of land uses within the MCSP (see below). It was the product of many lengthy discussions involving a broad cross section of citizens who volunteered to be involved in the planning exercise. Also included were the landowners. The "majority landowner" was the family who inherited the estate of Russell Bruzzone, who had built the Moraga Center after he had purchased the land from the Moraga Company in the 1960s.

Above, Moraga Center Specific Plan diagram; below, key opportunities and possible configuration of land uses (below). From 2002 Moraga General Plan, Ch. 8, pg. 2.

1 Shopping Center—potential redevelopment, redesign, intensification, or site improvements to create stronger pedestrian orientation

2 Under-utilized Land—potential for medium and medium-high density housing and/or commercial development

3 Potential extension of School Street

4 Proposed Town Center Facility Site

5 Creek and Moraga Ranch historic structures—development setbacks and potential linear park

6 Orchard Area—mixed-density housing, clustered to protect some of the orchard areas

7 Residential Area (3 units per acre; transition to existing neighborhoods)

8 Commercial/Office Areas (including existing assisted care facility, Moraga Barn, etc.)—some infill potential (small offices and/or housing)

9 "Limited Commercial" Area—some infill housing potential

The Moraga Center complex (see Area 1 in diagram of Specific Plan) is "Town & Country" style, which features single-story buildings with red-tile roofs, mostly interconnected. This style of architecture is outdated and tired. Many of the individual stores within the complex were old, some looked run-down. In the eyes of many Moragans, the place needed a major refurbishment. The property owner, on the other hand, refused to consider any ideas for improvement. He seemed of the opinion that the shopping center was just fine. The historic Moraga Ranch (see Area 5 in diagram), once the center of operations for the Moraga Company, was underutilized and in poor condition. Some would call it an example of urban blight. But the landowner insisted nothing was wrong. Along Laguna Creek on the west side of Areas 2 and 5 was fenced-in acreage on which numerous mobile homes sat, and where assorted items of construction equipment were scattered. Hardly anyone knew for certain what activities were taking place within this large and mostly gated compound.

Area 4, identified as the site of the proposed Town Center Facility, drew strong objections from the landowner, who refused to discuss the idea. This led to the town pursuing other alternatives. (See later information in this chapter on the Town Hall.)

Areas 6, 8, and 9 were candidates for medium-density housing, which could be student housing, workforce housing, or condominiums and apartment buildings. Area 8 had potential for congregate care facilities, assisted living uses, and condominium housing. Area 8 bordered Moraga Way and included the existing firehouse, several office buildings, and a large area suitable for clustered housing.

Area 7 was mostly owned by a separate landowner, who was interested in developing low-density housing (3 units per acre). He was agreeable to the town's suggestions, and, in the course of the negotiations, he dedicated 3.5 acres of vacant land in the northeast corner of Area 7 to the town. This land became West Commons Park, which connected to the Moraga Commons across Moraga Road. While a passive park, the sparsely improved parkland provides some enjoyment for Moraga citizens and visitors alike.

The MCSP represented considerable potential for improving a substantial area of underutilized land in the part of town traditionally considered the heart of Moraga. Much of what existed needed upgrading—both functionally and architecturally. The plan would open all manner of new opportunities, filling the needs of many citizens. The plan would make possible an inviting town center where people would like to spend time. Moreover, the MCSP represented Moraga's path to satisfying State-mandated housing requirements.[2] Some 600 dwelling units potentially could be provided within the MCSP area, if it was built out.

While the MCSP made sense to many citizens, not everyone welcomed the prospect of as many as 600 new homes clustered in the town center area. The thought of the increased traffic was more than many people could bear. Town staff spent considerable time analyzing the traffic impacts; they concluded that, given the kinds of housing proposed for the MCSP, the increases would be much less than an equivalent number of single-family dwellings, which is what the current zoning for the area allowed. In time, the objections subsided as more people realized the benefits outweighed the likely costs.

The major landowner, however, resisted nearly every suggestion made during the planning process. With only a few exceptions, he preferred not to develop. As a private landowner, that was his right. For this reason, much of what exists today in the MCSP area is exactly as it was at the time the MCSP was being formulated.

The landowner advanced the single project, and public reaction to the MCSP came into focus. A moderate-density housing complex of 36 attached townhouses was proposed by City Ventures on the lot between the fire station and existing office buildings on Moraga Way toward Orinda. The public outcry was loud and persistent. Traffic was one objection, but there were others. One young woman testified at a Town Council hearing that someone driving down Moraga Way toward Orinda would not be able to see the undeveloped ridgeline to the southwest beyond the Moraga Country Club and golf course. When asked why someone driving on Moraga Way would be preoccupied with ridgeline viewing, she was dumbfounded. The episode demonstrated that when some people really don't want something to happen, they'll throw all sorts of nonsense into the air. The project was approved, but not without a legal challenge by a disgruntled citizen that was dismissed by the court.

The MCSP was then, and remains to this day, an important path for improvement of the large expanse of land around the Moraga Center. As a matter of historical preservation, but also as a matter of improvement of the quality of life for many Moragans, the MCSP is a valuable guideline on how the area should be developed. Indeed, the MCSP formed the basis for detailed housing plans recently approved by the State as the town's housing element of the General Plan. While it may be the landowner's right to do with his land as he pleases, there comes a time when the citizens of the town can take matters into their own hands. They did it at the time of incorporation of the town, they could do it again. After all . . . All politics is local!

Financial Systems:
Overhauling Attitudes and Processes

When, as a planning commissioner, I was asked to participate in interviewing candidates for town manager in 2002, I became aware that Moraga's financial condition was not particularly healthy, and that the town had little ability to address the financial challenges that were apparent to nearly every one of the candidates. On the matter of budgets, one candidate remarked that Moraga's budget was little more than a list of things that the town would try and do in the coming year. There were no goals and objectives, there was no indication as to how things would be approached, and there were no indications about how success would be measured. The budget was just a list, nothing more.

At least one candidate remarked that the finance and administration department was not nearly what it needed to be. There were three individuals in the department. Two were local citizens whose jobs included such things as writing checks and maintaining the town's checking account. They were not full-time employees. The finance manager was a youngster fresh out of college. (It was revealed that this individual was the daughter of the town clerk.) None of the finance staff had any education in finance or accounting, and none had any experience in municipal finance. While they were all very charming people— who couldn't like them all?—none was qualified for their position.

The town treasurer was a citizen appointed by the Town Council who did nothing more than sign checks written against the town's checking account. He had no role whatsoever in overseeing the functions of the finance department. This seemed a waste. The treasurer could have been asked to do much more.

With respect to financing project expenditures, the town relied exclusively on grants. But there was no concerted effort to search for grant sources. Grants just appeared whenever some governmental program enacted a grant program. Winning a grant sometimes appeared to be a matter of luck. Occasionally, a grant just fell into the town's lap. There was no active program for raising funds through public financing, and it seemed no thought had been given to the opportunities that many other cities pursued regularly.

With respect to investment of town funds, this was a nonissue. The town collected what it could from the usual revenue sources (taxation and special grants); annual expenditures never exceeded projected annual revenues. There was never anything left to invest. The extent of the town's investment policy was to earn interest on the checking account balance.

On the matter of reporting to the public, there was very little. Anyone reading the town's financial reports would be able to identify revenues and expenditures, but no insight was provided as to whether spending was on track, ahead, or behind. In short, the public was kept in the dark, largely because the finance department had nothing to tell anyone. The town was also in the dark.

There was an annual audit, which was completed by a professional auditing firm. However, it wasn't clear what value could be gained from the audit function, other than to uncover evidence of fraud or embezzlement (which was never identified). Moreover, the auditor received little if any direction from the town. The auditor never interviewed the Town Council to see if there were any matters of concern to the council. Usually, auditors conduct such interviews, but not in Moraga. I'm not aware of any auditor's report to the Town Council that pointed out any of the more glaring deficiencies in the town's financial system.

In short, the department was essentially ineffective. On several occasions, citizens who had some qualifications in finance commented on this obvious deficiency. They regularly suggested that something should be done about it. It was clear none of these citizens appreciated being told there was nothing that could be done.

At a training forum conducted by the League of California Cities, I attended a session on financial management.[3] It was plain to me that much could be done with Moraga's financial management, but this would require a clean sweep of the existing department. At the forum, I was introduced to the idea of an audit and finance committee, whose function would be to oversee the municipal finances of the town. To my astonishment, I discovered that hardly any of the elected city representatives at the same training session had any idea of such a concept, even neighboring Lamorinda cities. This was amazing.

On return, I had a discussion with the new town manager, who clearly had become perplexed with the situation in the short while he'd been on the job. I pledged to support his recommendations to the Town Council for remedial measures. Fortunately, no one on the council objected to any of his ideas, and the town manager was given freedom to make things right. He started by hiring an experienced finance director, someone with genuine experience in public finance. After some initial hiccups, things began to change. The remainder of the staff were replaced with people with actual qualifications to do their jobs. Financial affairs began to run more professionally.

The Audit and Finance Committee (AFC) was established in 2007 comprising citizen volunteers and two council members. The oversight provided by the AFC helped the town manager assess the effectiveness of his finance department. The committee undertook studies of various financial matters relative to the town, which greatly helped the finance director and town manager formulate recommendations for new policies and procedures. The AFC interviewed auditing firms and recommended preferred companies competing to perform Moraga's annual audits; they also held sessions with the auditor and asked lots of questions. To the extent the auditors were free to do so, the AFC heard some excellent advice.[4]

The town treasurer was the chair of the AFC, and the position was filled by a citizen with demonstrated credentials in finance. One individual who was interviewed was holding the position of finance director at another city in Contra Costa County, and happened to be a Moraga resident. Other AFC members also had impressive credentials in finance and accounting, adding to the horsepower of this small oversight group.

The town manager instituted a program-oriented budgeting process, which built operating budgets based on goals and objectives set by the Town Council. While the initial process was a bit of an overkill for Moraga, the essence of the new process was eventually implemented in ways that made sense to everyone. Moreover, the public got to see what the town was doing through the lens of comprehensive budgeting.

The quality of financial reporting improved quickly, and concerned citizens were able to understand the town's finances as never before. The positive feedback was heartening. In 2013, the town was awarded a prize by the Government Finance Officers Association and was presented with a certificate for excellence in financial reporting and administration.[5] Moraga has won the same prize every year since then. It was amusing to listen to a council member of a neighboring town boast in 2016 that his town had just won this very prize; according to him, no other Contra Costa city or town had. I took great pleasure in informing this braggart privately that Moraga has won the prize three times already.[6]

As recently as December 2023, the town received an exemplary credit rating from Standard and Poor's, the global credit rating agency. This culminated the long trend toward financial stability that began in 2013 when the town issued debt instruments to finance a major townwide road repair program and acquisition of two buildings for the new Town Center (discussed later in this chapter). This exemplary rating affirmed Moraga's long-term financial stability. "The outlook is stable."[7]

Certificate of Achievement for Excellence showing ten consecutive years of award, 2013-2022. (Photo: Town of Moraga)

Revenue Enhancement

It didn't take long to realize that very little could be done to remedy some of the more glaring deficiencies in Moraga. This was plainly because the town couldn't afford to do much. Incredibly, the predominant view of many citizens was that the Town Council was spending money recklessly; the Town Council's consistent lament was "we can't afford it." Clearly this was going nowhere.

What also became clear as the town's finances were now more clearly in focus, was that the town didn't have an expenditure problem as much as a revenue problem. Traditionally, the town never spent more in any given year than it had on hand. It was a precise game of "pay as you go." It was also clear that to rectify this, no one had any idea what needed to be done, or in what order. Many citizens had all sorts of opinions, but none had any real concept of what was truly needed and, most important, how to pay for any of it. These were entirely uncharted waters for almost everyone.

Fortunately, a new town manager had been hired in 2008, a person of keen intellect and abundant common sense. He suggested to the council that a concerted effort be made to come to grips with Moraga's most serious dilemma: penury versus needs. In his short time on the job, the town manager had recognized that, while many people had opinions, hardly any of them knew what was really going on. What especially annoyed him was hearing over and again that Moraga government is a profligate spender. He knew this wasn't the case. So did several of us on the council. So, the manager suggested we form a special committee comprised of citizens who could rationally assess Moraga's needs and possible ways to finance them. Thus was born the Revenue Enhancement Committee (REC). Naturally, The Snipers caustically remarked that this was just a guise for disguising mismanagement and imposing new taxes. Nonetheless, the Town Council had the fortitude to push forward.

Revenue Enhancement Committee

The REC was commissioned to "recommend to the Town Council potential strategies for enhancing existing and creating new revenue sources [for general] and special purpose needs."[8] The committee was comprised of thirteen citizen volunteers (who represented a diverse range of professional talents and experiences), supported by a staff led by the town manager, the director of Administrative Services/Finance & Accounting, and the town engineer/director of the Public Works Department. Each of the citizen volunteers had credentials commensurate with the REC task, and each was committed to providing useful service.[9]

The committee comprised three subcommittees: Infrastructure, General Fund Revenues, and Economic Development. The Infrastructure group focused on street lighting, pavement conditions, storm drainage, buildings such as the library, and parks. The General Fund Revenue group considered a wide variety of taxation measures used by other cities to address problems like those plaguing Moraga. The Economic Development group addressed the long-term decline of the business centers, identifying reasons for the decline and ways to reverse the trend. This group focused on the economic potential of St. Mary's College, a thorough review of Moraga's regulations to make the town more business friendly, and proposing an economic development director who would focus on bringing new business to the town.

Working closely with town's staff, the REC reviewed the town's current financial condition and prospective needs. The review prompted the following statement on sustainability of the town's current financial condition:

> The town was established under the philosophical approach of a ***minimum service town*** and has adhered to that philosophy from a taxation and revenue standpoint. Not surprisingly, however, current expectations for services from the town have increased as new residents move in. While the town continues to maintain a balanced budget, its ability to fund its infrastructure needs and to improve services (such as police) has diminished. A declining sales tax base has exacerbated the town's revenue limitations. The compounding effect of this reduction in the revenue base, rising expectations, and deferral of infrastructure replacement has placed the town in a challenging position.[10] [Emphasis added.]

The committee further made findings that were not pleasant for many to hear. Quoting from the final report to the Town Council:[11]

1. Comparative municipal budget data show that Moraga receives substantially less in property tax and sales taxes per capita than the town's neighbors and other peer cities.

2. The town's operating reserves are minimal. Notwithstanding rigorous financial discipline, revenues and expenditures are currently on trend lines that may soon require severe service cutbacks. Moreover, because the town has not had the funding to properly maintain its roads and storm drains, both are deteriorating. Major action to halt that deterioration, stabilize both systems and ultimately return both to more satisfactory levels is needed immediately.

3. The town's two major shopping centers are no longer serving many of our town's most basic needs. This situation forces Moragans to do more and more of our shopping outside of our town. A direct effect of that situation has been a decline in the town's sales tax revenues.

The Town Council heard the report and discussed the recommendations. Of course, the Snipers mobilized and commenced firing shots, and the Tank appeared on several occasions to blast the council for trying to pull the wool over Moragans' eyes. None of this was productive. Nonetheless, the REC's findings were convincing to most people who listened carefully, and there appeared to be a swell of popular support for many of the REC's recommendations. It helped that the REC members were widely respected. It was also important that their work was being done with integrity—the local newspaper's reporter attended many of the work sessions of the study groups, and she paid close attention to what was being discussed. With that, the council authorized the next major step, which was to develop an action plan for addressing the issues identified by the REC.

Outreach to Neighborhoods

The Revenue Enhancement Committee's work set the stage for the next significant accomplishment: establish a baseline as to the community's knowledge of challenges facing the town, and what should be done to address them. The Town Council created a new committee called Revenue Enhancement Community Outreach to Neighborhoods (RECON), which included two council members (Howard Harpham and me), the REC chair (Dick Olsen), the Moraga Citizens Network chair (Ellen Beans), and the town manager (Mike Segrest). A management consultant was engaged pro bono from St. Mary's College (Dr. Larry Bienati).

A two-part approach was adopted. First, Dr. Bienati facilitated a series of focus group discussions, which were recorded by two experienced focus group recorders who were Moraga citizen volunteers. Six two-hour sessions were conducted, each with seven to ten focus group participants, representing a cross section of the town.[12] Each discussion followed the same plan, covering the same carefully constructed questions. The RECON committee's purpose was to listen and learn, not to discuss or advocate.[13]

The second part was an online survey, intending to validate the focus group discussions and to see if any additional issues surfaced. Dr. Bienati conducted this survey using his proprietary survey tool. A total of fifteen questions expanded the group's question list. Moragans were allowed about two weeks to respond online. By closing, 650 respondents had completed the survey. The results demonstrated the demographics of the online survey and the focus groups to be remarkably similar.[14]

Significant observations from the RECON program were that the focus group process was validated and reinforced by the online survey responses. Moragans had a compelling set of core values: quality schools, rural/quiet setting, safety, and parks and recreation; they wanted an enhanced retail environment and improved infrastructure maintenance; and they were prepared to invest in improving their community. But, it was up to the Town Council to demonstrate the value proposition, prioritize tax solutions, and provide credible expenditure plans. Finally, Moragans wanted multiple forms of communication dissemination to engage the community.[15]

In July 2010, RECON presented their report to the Town Council and a large crowd of attentive citizens. Dick Olsen, who was one of the citizens deeply involved in Moraga's incorporation in 1974, made the presentation. He shared his observation that Moragans' core values and expectations hadn't changed much in the thirty-five years since the incorporation. He closed his remarks with the following advice to the Town Council: "Now that you have your finger on the pulse of the community, keep it there."[16]

With that advice, the Town Council authorized planning a program for fixing Moraga's public streets.

Fixing Our Streets

RECON recognized that fixing Moraga's public streets would entail four principal tasks. First was to convince as many Moragans as possible that there was, indeed, a major problem with the streets. Second was designing a thorough engineering program and communicating the program to the public. Third was to develop a convincing financing strategy that would be acceptable to Moragans. And finally a political campaign was needed in order to carry the street repair program to the voters so they could have an opportunity to approve it—or deny it. RECON delved into this new effort right after the Town Council authorized the next phase to begin. The committee comprised members of the original RECON team, but for this phase of the work, a wide variety of special members were also engaged on short-term assignments. By the time of the general election in November 2012 (twenty-one months later), some thirty citizens and consultants had participated in this effort. Throughout the process, the committee reported to the Town Council frequently.

Moraga's Roads "At Risk"

Moraga's 56 miles of public roads are comprised of arterials (25 percent of the total mileage), which carry major traffic flow primarily into and out of town; and neighborhood streets (75 percent), which convey traffic to arterials throughout the neighborhoods of the town. Not included are the private streets in private communities such Sanders Ranch and the

Country Club. The town is responsible for the public roads; private neighborhoods take care of their own streets.[17]

For some time, the town engineer had been regularly assessing the condition of the public road system. Using an analytical tool called "StreetSaver," the town's pavement consultant surveyed every mile of public streets. Conditions were reported in terms of a parameter known as the Pavement Condition Index.[18] As of November 2011, the majority of arterials were in Good condition or better; nearly a quarter of the arterial streets were considered Fair/At Risk; and nearly 20 percent were in Poor or worse condition. By contrast, neighborhood streets were in much worse condition: over half were graded as Failed or Poor; 20 percent were Fair/At Risk; and only 20 percent were in Good condition or better.

To the question, "What if we do nothing for neighborhood roads?" the shocking prediction was that over a ten-year period, close to three quarters of them would have failed, 13 percent would have deteriorated to Poor, 12 percent would be Fair/At Risk, but only 3 percent would be in Good condition. What's more, the conditions of neighborhood streets were evenly distributed all over the town, confirming that this was a townwide problem. Furthermore, bad omens could be found; for instance, the condition of one arterial road (Rheem Blvd., as shown in the photo between St. Mary's Road and Moraga Road) was such that fire trucks could not travel on the damaged pavement without risk of sustaining damage.[19]

A failed road, Rheem Blvd., south end, 2007. (Photo: Town of Moraga Public Works)

As to the question "Why are we in this predicament?" several reasons were obvious. Operating revenues were consumed by essential services like police and public works (basic utilities, and other things such as tree trimming). Since projected revenues were flat, there were no prospects of funds for fixing streets other than for major roads, which is where most grant monies could be used. Except for a very few larger neighborhood streets (so-called collectors), nothing remained to fix the rest of the neighborhood streets, and there were no reserve funds that could be applied to street maintenance. Indeed, Moraga was a "Minimum Services Town" . . . and that was plain.

The REC committee had demonstrated that Moraga spent less money per capita than any of its peer cities in Contra Costa County. There were no prospects for increases in tax revenues from either property taxes or economic activity. This was why many other cities were turning to new forms of taxation to fund their street repair programs. This message was not received favorably by everyone: While some difficult persons insisted that the REC findings were bogus, more rational people realized that, yes, there was a problem . . . and, yes, something needed to be done, soon.

At one information meeting with the Moraga Lions Club in 2011, two RECON members shared the findings of the road studies completed thus far. The focus of the discussion was on deteriorating roads and on the town's inability to do something about it. Reactions to the discussions indicated genuine interest in what was being said, and most listeners understood that there was a real problem that needed urgent attention. But the naysayers were there. According to a reporter who was attending, one individual remarked "In fact, you are coming to meet all the groups in town to sell the voters." To this, Howard Harpham of RECON remarked, "We are here to inform you of the reality of our infrastructure. . . . What will be done about it will be your decision."[20]

Information session with the Moraga Lions Club. Left to right, Lion Dan Hagen, Jill Keimach, Howard Harpham, and Lion Dana Glasgow. (Photo: Sophie Braccini)

Such information meetings were held with many different organizations. The work in delivering the RECON message never seemed to end. But people were listening. It was now time to develop a townwide plan for neighborhood street maintenance, based on a funding strategy that was comprehensive, fair, and long term. Notwithstanding a small group of detractors, most Moragans appeared to accept that the time had come. They embraced a positive attitude: Local problems require local solutions . . . It's up to us!

Engineering Solution

The next task was to formulate an engineering program with scenarios for improving At Risk neighborhood streets. "StreetSaver" was used to generate various pavement repair scenarios over a ten-year horizon, generating cost estimates for possible annual programs. An important result was that it was much cheaper to maintain good roads than to rebuild failed ones. This supported the argument that it's better to maintain relatively high average pavement conditions and attend to those in poorer condition as funds are available. Whatever the selected program, the costs were going to be substantial—many millions of dollars—and new funding strategies would need to be identified.

Most Moragans who listened carefully to RECON's preliminary findings were willing to accept them, albeit not happily. Contrarians emerged, as expected. The usual suspects arrived to criticize and poke holes in RECON's recommendation. The Know-It-All folks forcefully registered their opinions on what should be done: "This is what you should do!" The Think-They-Know-It-Alls suggested alternatives, demonstrating very little real understanding of the fundamental engineering principles of pavements. And there was the negativity offered by the No crowd, who couldn't imagine that something so serious as fixing Moraga streets for millions of dollars could ever be done. Yet, everyone needed to be heard. Some good ideas might emerge; some potential helpers might be identified. After all, Moragans could be asked to vote on a funding measure sometime soon.

Financing a Multi-Year Program

To a great extent, the engineering strategy would be driven by the funding strategy that would be pursued, and the funding strategy would be aimed at what Moraga voters would accept. Several citizens with broad experience in finance added expertise in financing methods. Several had experience with public indebtedness; one was a public finance attorney. These new additions brought valuable insights to the team, and they helped sort through the smorgasbord of revenue enhancement alternatives that had been identified earlier by the Revenue Enhancement Committee. Potential approaches were reduced to a few. The conclusion was that debt would be unavoidable and that a new tax would be necessary to service the debt. The most viable approach was a 1 percent sales tax that would be added to the State Sales Tax that had been in place for years. The municipal finance experts suggested use of Certificates of Participation (COPs), which would likely be well received in the financial marketplace.[21]

Various pavement repair program scenarios were tested with COP financing. The conclusion was that twenty-year program would require an intensive three-year pavement program to address the most critical At Risk streets ($7.7 million), which would incur $600,000 in annual debt interest expense. The COP would be serviced by $1 million annual sales tax proceeds from a new 1 percent sales tax levy.[22]

The Town Council heard RECON's recommendations in late 2011. After discussion, the council realized that it would be a difficult sell to Moragans, who were notoriously averse to public debt (unless it was debt for any of the public schools). The council then authorized proceeding with a ballot measure to be contested in the November 2012 general election. That was the RECON team's next challenge.

Measure K

RECON engaged a professional elections consultant who had broad experience with Northern California elections for public financing proposals. The consultant predicted that passing any revenue measure would be challenging, so a telephone survey of likely Moraga voters was conducted by a pollster to assess this presumption. The survey was not encouraging: A simple majority might possibly be realized for any measure involving indebtedness, but under no circumstances could a supermajority (more than two-thirds of voters) approval be expected.[23] The pollster also determined that voters would not accept any proposal that did not have a "sunset" provision (a setting of a definite life of the tax); and that voters expected a citizen oversight provision to ensure that Morgans were getting what they voted for. This information clearly indicated a ballot measure for a "general tax" with limited duration, and creation of an oversight committee to be formed once the measure passed.

In July 2012, the Town Council passed a resolution calling an election to ask Moraga voters to approve a twenty-year General Transactions and Use Tax of one cent. The resolution authorized preparation of a written argument and rebuttal in favor of the proposed measure; it also authorized expenditure of funds necessary to place the measure on the election ballot.[24] The Town Council directed RECON to proceed with initiating a campaign to be conducted by a citizen group separate from the Town of Moraga government.[25] The county election department advised the town that the ballot measure would be identified as "Measure K—Town of Moraga."[26] The Argument in Favor of Measure K was signed by a former mayor of the town (who was a member of the town's founding committee in the 1970s), two business owners, a longtime resident (who had been a member of the Revenue Enhancement Committee), and by me (as then-current mayor). No Argument Against Measure K was received by the county, which was a pleasant surprise, so no rebuttal was necessary.

The Yes on Measure K campaign committee was formed right away. Chairing the committee was John Hafner, a longtime resident and well-known volunteer through the local Kiwanis Club of Moraga Valley, who led a large contingent of other citizens.[27] A full-blown campaign was designed, and volunteers from all over town chipped in. The usual paraphernalia (yard signs, media ads, etc.) were designed, and pamphlets were prepared for a band of advocates who would cover Moraga neighborhoods in a closely coordinated program of knocking on doors, distributing information, and talking to fellow citizens. A robust speakers' bureau was formed to coordinate committee members delivering a standard presentation and responding to citizen questions. Over a two-month period, RECON speakers meet with service clubs in their regular meeting venues and with citizen groups in their homes. A citizen volunteer, who was an amateur filmmaker, produced a delightful short film that told a story, saying, in part:

> *Once upon a time . . . there was a very nice town called Moraga*
> *But soon an evil force began to invade this lovely town: POTHOLES!*
> *What was Moraga to do?*
> *Was this the end of the little town of Moraga?*
> *Or did they band together and rid their town of POTHOLES?*
> *IT'S UP TO YOU!*
> *Join us in voting Yes on K*
> *Knock out POTHOLES!*

The local theater operator agreed to show the film in the Rheem Theater before each feature-film screening. Five minutes long, the film was carefully scripted, tastefully humorous, and professionally produced. It brought smiles to many of those who saw it, while delivering the important message:

> *It's time to rid Moraga of Potholes! Vote for Measure K.*

Did these efforts work? They must have. Measure K passed with 70.5 percent of the vote, far better than a supermajority that the professional pollster said could not be won. The tally was Yes - 5,993; No - 2,505.

Another demonstration of local politics in action.

Town Hall: What's Needed and Affordable

At the time of incorporation, Moraga conducted official business in the Casita building at the Hacienda de las Flores. After a short while, the town offices were moved to 350 Rheem, largely because the Police Department needed a more appropriate headquarters. Some other town functions moved to the same building. This arrangement continued until the landlord asked the town to vacate the premises in order to make room for the expanding needs of a special-needs school, which occupied the same building complex. The Police Department moved to an office building on School Street, close to the Moraga Center; other town functions moved back into the Hacienda main building. This entire arrangement was unsatisfactory.

Since incorporation, the Public Works Department had maintained its corporation yard on the Hacienda property, in the wooden grove across Laguna Creek from the Pavilion, accessed from Moraga Road. The operations within this yard had long been a concern for environmental reasons, since potential pollution from the corporation yard could enter Laguna Creek, which flows from Campolindo (Laguna de los Palos Colorados) to the San Leandro reservoir south of town.

Also since incorporation, the town had been conducting public meetings of the Town Council and the Planning Commission, which usually drew large audiences, in the auditorium at Joaquin Moraga Intermediate School. This had worked well for years. But then televising these meetings became a serious consideration, at the urging of many citizens wanting greater transparency in public affairs. However, the school was in no position to guarantee the security of the town's video equipment. This eliminated the prospect of televising meetings from the auditorium.

Since adopting the General Plan 2002, the concept of a town center was in many minds. Several on the Town Council thought a perfect location would be vacant land across Moraga Road from the Moraga Commons, which was included in the potential land use allocation for the Moraga Center Specific Plan (as mentioned earlier—see Area 4 in the MCSP Map). However, the property owner refused to consider the idea. Then attention turned to vacant land behind the veterinarian clinic opposite the Rheem Center. But the veterinarian, who owned the building that would have to be demolished, demanded terms unacceptable to the Town Council. Finally, a relatively new building at 329 Rheem Blvd. came on the market. This was a two-story office building which the Town Council thought would be splendid for town offices, including the police headquarters. So, the Town Council purchased the building, with the intention to remodel the building as a Town Hall.

While the building seemed to be in good condition, problems surfaced as the re-modeling came to grips with its true state. The building had been built to minimum standards, and as inexpensively as possible. But the most serious issue was that its structural integrity was deficient from a seismic risk standpoint. No police department (or any other critical operation) would be allowed into the building without major seismic retrofit work. This was a shock. Nonetheless, the renovation work proceeded, and elements of town staff began to occupy the building in 2008 while remodeling was underway.

Moraga Town Offices and Police Headquarters, 2009. (Town of Moraga file photo)

Close to 329 Rheem Blvd. was a vacant fire station that MOFD had abandoned when the Fire District built their new station on Moraga Road. The building resembled a two-vehicle garage with a wide-open interior. The Town Manager suggested to the Town Council a project for multi-use of the property: a corporation yard in the rear, offices for public works staff in a small area in the front, and a large meeting room that could accommodate about fifty people. The building could also serve as an emergency operations center, and televising meetings would now be possible. The manager also devised a financing scheme that required a modest loan (Certificate of Participation), and the sale of some miscellaneous surplus town property.

The proposal made sense to the Town Council, but it brought out the No people who were concerned with financial feasibility. One of them asked, "There is only one question. Can we afford it?" Another citizen was much more negative: "We can't do it, we know we can't; we have the potential, but we don't have the money. Don't raise everybody's taxes to pay for your dreams."[28] As the council discussed the proposal, it became clear that the plan made sense for many operational reasons. Moreover, the town manager's financing scheme was imaginative and was affordable, if executed carefully as a low-cost project. The proposal was approved, and the old fire station became the multi-purpose facility for Council Chambers and public meetings, a field operation center, and the town's Emergency Operations Center.

"It's definitely low budget, Moraga way," said Jill Keimach, the town manager who oversaw completion of the remodel of the 329 and 335 Rheem Blvd. buildings.[29] By the fall of 2012, all town departments had moved into 329 Rheem Blvd.; Parks and Recreation remained in the Hacienda, which by then was entirely available for the town's recreation purposes, just as had been intended in 1973, when the property was purchased from the Christian Brothers. Refurbishment of 335 Rheem Blvd. was completed in October 2015, and soon after, televised public meetings were launched in the new Town Council Chambers there.[30]

What worked well in this project? First and foremost, a succession of excellent town managers had the acumen to make it happen, financially, architecturally, and in terms of frugal project management. Second, the Town Council had the good sense to give competent staff the freedom to act; while the staff was kept on a tight leash, they were not second-guessed. Third, the press remained friendly, writing simple, concise, and honest pieces throughout the lengthy project. Lastly, Moragans were beginning to realize that Moraga could do some important things and do them in imaginative ways. Their pride in their super-frugal Town Hall was palpable.

Playgrounds in the Parks

Moraga's reputation for excellent parks is well-earned. The earliest Moraga land barons and developers had promoted their dreams of public parks that would enhance the lives of those who lived in the town they imagined. After the town purchased the 40-acre parcel from the State in 1978, the Moraga Commons was born. The park was dedicated in 1982 as Moraga's largest multi-use park. Since then, improvements over the years have been the fruits of individuals and public groups striving to provide recreation amenities for their fellow citizens. The band shell was built in the 1980s largely by community donations, and it has since been used for all manner of activities drawing very large crowds for annual events such as the Summer Concert series, the Moraga Pear Festival, and on July Fourth. The park contains picnic areas, volleyball courts, half-basketball courts, and playground facilities for children. The playgrounds deserve mention here as examples of things that went well in the town.

Lamorinda Skatepark

Beginning around the year 2000, the Town Council decided to try to build a skatepark within Moraga Commons. A site on a hillside adjacent to Moraga Road was identified, and conceptual designs were prepared. Public enthusiasm was high. But the financial picture in town in those days ruled out any prospect that Moraga could carry out a project such as this. Wisely, a regional approach was pursued, and Lafayette and Orinda agreed to join Moraga in funding what would become the Lamorinda Skatepark.

The skatepark was opened in 2003 and became a popular place for young skateboarders to learn and practice their skills in a well-designed and well-built skateboarding facility. Moraga was responsible for operations and security, which carried all manner of challenges as usage increased and some less-than-responsible individuals kept Moraga public works and police busy policing and cleaning up vandalism. Security fencing was installed, which improved things a bit, but the skatepark remained a burden for the town. Nonetheless, a parking lot was added (another joint city project), and the skatepark continued to grow as a welcome public attraction. There was no desire to curtail it; instead, residents learned to live with it. To this day, the skatepark remains a very popular place.

Moraga Commons Playgrounds

During the 1990s, two tot lots were constructed within the Commons. The structures were marginal affairs, constructed of timber, and not especially kidproof. Through the efforts of the Moraga Kiwanis Club, the structures in the largest of the two lots were replaced with new structures made of steel and durable plastic; the smaller lot's structures were replaced by the Rotary Club with ones of the same caliber as those in the larger lot. Both projects required community contributions and major construction efforts by citizens who wanted the playgrounds of the highest quality possible. Both projects were completed in 2006.

The Moraga Rotary Club then undertook a major project to build an all-access playground—the first of its kind in Lamorinda—for children of all abilities. The playground had twenty-four separate elements all designed to be compatible with the needs of children with various physical and emotional challenges, with enough variety that the playground would be inviting for children of all abilities to play together. The estimated cost (approximately $250,000) was much higher than the Rotary Club had anticipated, yet the Rotarians raised the funds through a vigorous campaign canvassing citizens and service groups throughout town. They also worked with Benioff Children's Hospital of Oakland to ensure that the facility would be appropriately designed and built.

Location of the all-access playground was a contentious matter. Rotarians originally planned to situate it at Rancho Laguna Park on the southeast end of town, which would have been the least expensive option. However, competing interests for space at that park suggested that the playground should be at Moraga Commons. Then a concerned group of citizens claimed that the Commons could not accommodate the large all-access facility. This wasn't so. There was sufficient space. Provided that the project could bear the costs of extensive site preparation, Moraga Commons would be the best location. The Town Council agreed, and, notwithstanding the additional costs, encouraged the Moraga Rotary Club to think in terms of the Moraga Commons location. That's where the all-access playground was built, beginning with site planning in 2015. In 2018, the playground opened to the delight of many children and their families, and it has since become a popular regional attraction. It is splendid.

All three playground projects at Moraga Commons demonstrated the power of public service by Moragans. They inspired the projects, raised most of the money to make them happen, and lent their own labor and expertise to the constructions. The projects also demonstrated the ability of the Town of Moraga to facilitate making things happen . . . to make decisions that promoted rather than impeded progress. Moragans were better off for it all.

Veterans Memorial

A small group of veterans proposed that a memorial be constructed at Moraga Commons to honor those Moragans who had given their lives in service to their country. John Haffner, a retired naval officer, learned that a young Moragan named Tony Knox—an Eagle Scout candidate with one of the local troops of Boy Scouts of America—was looking for a suitable service project for his Eagle Scout award. This gave rise to the concept of a veteran's memorial located at Moraga Commons. After discussion with the Parks and Recreation Director and a few members of the Town Council, a site was identified near the flagpole at the Commons' entrance at Moraga Road and St. Mary's Road. The memorial would be a large rock, three feet tall and four feet wide, set near where a public trail crosses the Commons and leads to the entrance, with an engraving set into the rock that would identify all the uniformed military services of the United States. The idea was brought to the Town Council and was approved without objection. Tony Knox organized funding with donations from the Moraga Park Foundation, local service clubs, and generous individuals who wanted this memorial to be built. Tony coordinated the construction. The inaugural celebration was conducted on Veterans Day, 2010. Every year since then, Veterans Day has been honored with a brief and tasteful event conducted at the Moraga Veterans Memorial.[31]

Moraga Veterans Memorial (Photo: Town of Moraga files)

Mayor Dave Trotter addresses attendees at Moraga Veterans Day, 2013
*(Photo: David Mills/*Lamorinda Patch)

Sports Fields

Moraga is a place of hills and valleys, mostly hills. Most development is in the valleys or on hillsides, occupying most of the flat spaces of the valley. When the schools were formed, the flat land in the immediate vicinity of each school was taken by the school districts. Naturally, school districts used the flat land for playgrounds or sports fields. The town had control over very little other land that was suitable for playing fields.

Moraga is also a place where organized sports are popular, particularly youth sports. Playing fields are always in short supply, and the town has always had an interest in opportunities to acquire suitable land for these purposes, or to secure funding to make improvements to existing fields. The school districts are obvious places to find fields, and the schools have traditionally done what they can to accommodate the public need by permitting public use of their fields. The town has always tried to help wherever possible, usually in terms of funding for field maintenance, and occasionally when funding opportunities appeared in terms of grants. Such an opportunity arose in 2008, when the East Bay Regional Park District (EBRPD) advertised that Measure WW grants were available to cities for improving sports fields for public usage.

At a joint meeting of the Town Council and Moraga School District, the town addressed the prospect of seeking—and winning—a Measure WW grant. The School District sensed an opportunity to improve their sports fields, and the Town Council agreed to study the opportunities within the inventory of fields to which Measure WW grant funds might apply. A committee was appointed comprising two Town Council members (which included Dave Trotter and me), two School Board members, the school superintendent, the town manager, and representatives from the Moraga Sports Alliance (which coordinated public use of school playing fields through the School District).

Beginning in June 2009, an inventory of potential sites for the fields was developed. Of six sites, four were existing playing fields owned by the School District, one was a parcel of undeveloped school land, and the last was the town's Rancho Laguna Park on the southeast corner of town. In the monthly meetings that followed, proposed improvements for each site were discussed, and the potential for each project meeting Measure WW criteria was assessed. A few of the projects were minor, one was very large, and several were projects that might qualify. The major hurdles that needed to be met were project cost (limited to $737,750) and open access to the completed project for general public use.

The town organized all engineering and planning, and the town manager and school superintendent tackled matters of public usage and long-term maintenance. As project definitions were completed, rebuilding and expanding the existing playing fields at the Camino Pablo School clearly had the most promise. The project would include two Little League baseball fields plus a rectangular field for multiple configurations of grid sports, backstops, bleachers, and fencing. At a joint meeting of the Town Council and School Board in October 2009, the proposed project was confirmed, and terms for public usage and maintenance were outlined. The town was authorized to pursue Measure WW grant funding, and to prepare a license agreement with the School District authorizing the town to make improvements to the fields and to permit open public usage of the school property. Both the town and the district worked cooperatively, and a license agreement was approved in February 2010.

The EBRPD approved Moraga's Measure WW grant application, and, in early 2011, the project was underway. The Camino Pablo sports field was dedicated in a ceremony on December 8, 2011.

This success surprised many citizens. Rarely had the town and the School District agreed on any such cooperative project, and to do it in so short a time was unimaginable. One of the Sports Alliance representatives remarked that he'd had little faith that a deal could ever be done. But a deal in fact was completed, thanks to excellent collaboration between the town manager and school superintendent. Both governing boards were pleased with the outcome. It was a rare and welcome demonstration of goodwill and perseverance.

The project succeeded because those appointed to the committee were determined to make it happen. Both governing bodies had the good sense to allow the committee to work freely and without overbearing supervision. And a grateful public (with the exception of a few of the usual negative detractors), supported the process from start to finish. That the public was included at every step did a lot to build trust that good things would be delivered.

Joint Facilities Planning

In 2013, on the heels of the successful Measure K campaign and the completion of the Camino Pablo sports field renovation project, the Town Council and School Board jointly decided it was time to address the wider matter of public usage of town and district facilities, not just sports fields. Both governing boards were optimistic that there could be many public benefits from a joint study of opportunities. This gave rise to the Joint Facilities Planning Subcommittee, whose members would be two Town Council members (Dave Trotter and me), two School Board members, a Moraga Parks and Recreation Department commissioner, representatives of Campolindo High School and St. Mary's College, four representatives of youth sports organizations in town, the town manager and the superintendent of schools. The purpose of the subcommittee was to develop recommendations on ways that the town, School District, Campolindo High School, and St. Mary's College could partner through existing facilities and develop a plan to improve those facilities.

From February 2014 until January 2015, the subcommittee met monthly. The initial task was create a thorough inventory of all facilities used by the owners and the public. It was perhaps the only time this had ever been done. While demonstrating the extent of current public uses, constraints on usage, and known opportunities for facility improvement, the process also highlighted problems with shared usage and pointed out opportunities where administration of facility user organizations could be made better. The group constructed a considerable matrix of potential sites and types of facilities that would help meet mutual needs.

From extensive consideration of ideas, the subcommittee concluded that the town had a genuine need for more turf playing fields (grid sports as opposed to diamond sports), more gymnasium space, and a community center. Two major projects emerged as having the most potential: a conversion of Hacienda de las Flores into a multi-generational community center facility; and the construction of a gymnasium and the improvements of the existing turf fields at Joaquin Moraga Intermediate School. Concept-level cost estimating indicated that either of these paths would require significant capital infusion, but would go a long way toward satisfying some of Moraga's recreation needs. However, the subcommittee concluded that it made no sense to proceed further without professional help from sports and recreation facility developers.

The School District representatives then informed the subcommittee that the district was in the process of strategic planning. Apparently, the district had concluded that expansion of Moraga population in the coming decade would translate to expansions in the schools, and therefore, it was not in the district's interests to commit any present school properties to any of the potential uses identified by the subcommittee. This indicated the Joaquin Moraga Intermediate School project could proceed no further.[32]

Campolindo High School (which is just one of four campuses of the Acalanes Union High School District) declined to commit to any of the potential projects identified by the subcommittee. Their reasoning was that should they do something like any of these projects for Moraga, they would be obliged to do similarly for Lafayette, Orinda, and Walnut Creek, where other AUHSD campuses were situated.

St. Mary's College also declined to become involved in any of the projects involving the college. Strategic planning, which was currently in progress, indicated that college needs would preclude further town usage of college facilities. The college preferred to remain with the status quo.

In a joint meeting in January 2015, the subcommittee reported the results of their efforts to the Town Council and School Board. It was clear that no further progress could be made as a joint effort; each of the four bodies should pursue their own plans for the future.[33]

While it was disappointing that no specific project initiative had emerged from the eleven-month planning exercise, the entire venture had been worthwhile. From the process, each of the four bodies developed better understandings of the needs and aspirations of the others. Some attractive projects were identified, and it had become clear how some of them might be pursued. Moreover, the entire process demonstrated that the four bodies could work collaboratively, which is not something that always happens.

With that, the subcommittee was disbanded, and Moraga undertook the concept study of Hacienda de las Flores that had been suggested.

CHAPTER 7

Things That Didn't

NOT ALL THINGS WENT WELL—not by a long shot. There were several disappointments over the years and some utter failures. But it's worth noting these instances and examining what went wrong. Perhaps things could have been done differently and better outcomes might have been realized. On the other hand, some situations simply had no chance of ending differently.

This chapter looks at some of the things undertaken during my tenure as a Moraga planning commissioner and as Town Council member (1999-2016) that didn't go well at all. Some good things came from some of the efforts, but at the end of the day, it can't be said that any were successes. Sadly, the episodes created opportunities for difficult people to be at their worst, and our failures to handle these people in a different manner had much to do with the unhappy outcomes. After several of these unfortunate episodes, I had to wonder whether it was all worth the effort.

Rancho Laguna Dog Park:
Special Versus General Interests

This 8.4-acre park on the southeast corner of the town was acquired by Moraga in 1979 as a buffer between the town and the unincorporated territory beyond. It was named Rancho Laguna Park and was intended to be a minimally developed, passive park. Some minor improvements were made to the park in the early years. A modest playground and picnic facilities were built, and a campfire site with rustic amphitheater was configured for occasional camping adventures by groups such as local scout organizations. Mainly, the park was an open space for solitude, peace, contemplation, and relaxation.[1]

Rancho Laguna Park, looking east, showing off-leash dog running.
(*Photo:* Bay Area Telegraph, *April 2023*)

But the park had also become a place where people would let their dogs run freely off-leash, which they had done there for nearly thirty years. People exercised their dogs daily and largely without heed to the town's off-leash restrictions, though signage regarding the rules was posted prominently. Some dog owners had little control over their animals; some dogs were not well mannered. Dog owners seemed to regard the place as a dog park. However, the town had received numerous complaints about dogs bothering picnic goers, snatching food, and sometimes causing a ruckus. There also were reports of instances of dogs allegedly assaulting children. Though, over the years, no incidents were reported that involved serious injury caused by misbehaving dogs, it was felt that something had to be done.

The spacious grounds of the park had also become popular for casual sports. A group of citizens who were soccer enthusiasts attempted to organize a youth soccer program on the park grounds. This posed a conflict between soccer folks and dog-parkers (as they were called by some). The arguments turned ugly in a hurry, and it wasn't long before the Town Council was dragged into the fray. There seemed no willingness of one party to accommodate the other, so the town felt obliged to make rules. At first, a "temporal separation" solution was tried, where off-leash hours would be limited to certain times of the day, and general use to the other hours. But that was hardly enforceable since Moraga police were not staffed to implement such a regulation.

Then a "spatial separation" solution was proposed: a fence to divide the park into dog- and non-dog areas. After much deliberation, the town introduced a plan that would partition the park with fencing, creating a dog park about 1.1 acre in size, a fenced-in playground, and a large open space for general uses. This drew a barrage of complaints from the dog-parkers, who threatened legal action against the town to enjoin any such partitioning. They even invoked an endangered species—the Dusky-footed Wood Rat—as being threatened by the presence of the town's proposed fencing.[2] So, the town passed an ordinance that restricted off-leash dog-running to certain hours for at least a year, until a dedicated dog park could be created somewhere. The upshot of this was a petition signed by 20 percent of Moraga voters calling for a popular vote on whether the ordinance would be maintained or rescinded.[3]

At this same time the campaign for Measure K (see Chapter 6 reference to fixing Moraga roads) was getting underway. The Town Council was fully invested in passage of Measure K, and the prospect of a companion question on the same ballot was risky. One council member wisely noted, ". . . although political decisions are made about ideas, emotions must be taken into account. . . . [If] people were to see a tax measure to support the [road repair program] and a referendum about supporting a fenced dog park on the same ballot, they could unconsciously establish a connection between the two. . . . We are human beings, we are not always logical; we have feelings and feelings always win."[4] The council voted 3-2 to rescind the restriction of the off-leash ordinance.

The Town Council then faced what seemed an unresolvable dilemma. While the dog park matter was of high importance to many, there were other more pressing issues facing the council—namely fixing Moraga's streets. Clearly, it was best not to try and solve the dog park problem, at least not at that time. If citizens didn't want to coexist with other peoples' pets, there wasn't much the town could do about it—for sure, imposing onerous ordinances or carving up a beautiful park wasn't going to work. So, the Town Council dropped the matter entirely. The interest of the dog-parkers trumped the interest of the soccer folks; the picnickers and others who didn't like out-of-control dogs were the losers. There seemed to be no other choice.

This controversy demonstrated difficult people at their worst on all sides of the argument. Public meetings on the subject of Rancho Laguna Park were generally unpleasant affairs, where uncivil behavior and ad hominem attacks were the norm. Some of the dog-parkers couldn't restrain their emotions and let their animosities flow forth. At one meeting, an especially irate individual—a well-known Grenade—stormed out of the auditorium screaming obscenities that hadn't been heard in a Town Council meeting in recent memory. At another meeting, jeering got out of hand, but the local police presence helped calm things down. It was a dispiriting time, so bad that one of the Town Council members decided not to run for re-election. Another suffered re-election defeat, perhaps on account of her position opposing the dog-parkers.[5]

How could this unfortunate episode have been handled better? It would have helped if there had been a more earnest—and much earlier—attempt to discuss the agenda of the dog-parkers with them. There might have been a path forward that comported with their self-interests. What was clear was that public reaction to local government imposing rules that did not have broad public appeal was simply a nonstarter.

One happy outcome of the controversy was the Rancho Laguna playground, which was within one of the fenced-in areas that was part of the Town's partitioning plan. The play structures that had been erected some twenty years earlier were deemed unsafe for children; they had been constructed of timber and had deteriorated to the point where replacement was necessary. Through the efforts of several local service clubs, funds were raised to purchase new playground equipment of similar quality to that installed at Moraga Commons several years earlier. A joint project between Kiwanis and Rotary created the Rancho Laguna playground, which was dedicated in the summer of 2012.

Speed Bumps: A Real Screw-Up

In the summer of 2007, a pavement restoration project was completed on Camino Pablo, one of the major streets (arterials) in town. This project was the first time the street had ever been refurbished beyond simple pothole repairs. Public appreciation and expectations were high. When the smooth new pavement was complete, the 1.2-mile-long, extra-wide and nearly straight street was more like an airfield runway than a small-town street. People were delighted to soar down the roadway at amazing speeds. However, the street passed by two schools (Camino Pablo Elementary and Joaquin Moraga Intermediate School), so speeding vehicles were an understandable concern. With school opening in a few weeks, the town engineer proposed that crosswalks at the schools be "slightly raised to increase visibility and differentiate them from the roadway." Whether such crosswalks would be called "raised crosswalks," speed bumps, or speed tables was beside the point; they were intended to slow traffic to 15 miles per hour. Three speed bumps were constructed across the new pavement (two at Camino Pablo School and one at JM Intermediate School). But they weren't "slightly raised," they were 12" high with steep slopes on either side.

The public outcry was immediate and loud. Moraga police investigated several accident scenes where autos had taken the speed bumps at high speed. One vehicle was reported to have become airborne and crashed on landing. Another suffered a smashed oil pan when the vehicle smashed onto the pavement having jumped a speed bump. Another story was told of a driver who routed his car thorough the JM parking lot just to avoid having to go over the speed bump in front of the school. That the driver's detour put children walking in the parking lot at risk didn't seem to matter. Clearly, the speed bumps were encouraging bad behavior. Certainly, they were not serving their intended purpose.

By then, summer vacations ended and school was back in session, so Moragans—not just a few people, but nearly the entire town—turned their attention to making sure the speed bumps were corrected. Some wanted them removed entirely. Town Council meetings became the public forum in which the council was pilloried for allowing these obstructions to be built in the first place. Original intentions didn't matter. Protesters just didn't like them. Informal surveys were conducted by groups of citizens showing split public opinion: about half the people—those with children in the schools and those who didn't regularly use Camino Pablo—didn't mind the speed bumps at all; the other half—primarily those who did not have children in the schools, and those who used the road frequently—violently objected to any bumps. At the time, there appeared to be no compromise.[6]

The matter was ultimately decided by MOFD, who pointed out that a fully stocked ambulance could not negotiate a speed bump at more than a crawl without damage to the ambulance, its contents, and possibly its occupants. A similar situation existed for a fully loaded water tender fire truck. MOFD performed road tests and determined that the three speed bumps added nearly fifteen minutes to the response time for an emergency vehicle traveling the 1.2-mile stretch of Camino Pablo from Canyon Road to Sanders Ranch. The discussion then became one of life and death. One distressed parent, who was a resident in Sanders Ranch, testified that the life of his son, who was suffering from a physical condition featuring seizures, depended on rapid ambulance response.

That testimony convinced several of my colleagues and me that a mistake had been made. So we proposed to remove the speed bumps with an apology for not having cleared the original plan with MOFD.[7] At the time, I was the mayor, so it fell to me to deliver a public mea culpa. The Town Council had made a mistake. It was appropriate to admit it, correct it, and move on.[8]

TSAC: Not All Good Ideas Fly

Throughout my professional life, I have always been involved in organizational safety, first in the Navy, then on construction projects with Chevron. Safety was always foremost in the operations in which I was involved. It seemed I always gravitated to the safety groups of the organizations where I worked, so it was no surprise that I was drawn to safety issues in Moraga.

Many Moragans complained about the unsafe driving practices of other Moragans, citing all sorts of bad driving behavior. Many of these complaints were justified; a lot of Moragans were unsafe drivers. When I became a council member, I spent time with the police chief, becoming familiar with the challenges facing his department. At the top of his list of concerns was traffic safety. His small police force was in no position to do as much traffic enforcement and safe driving education as was appropriate for a community of 16,500 residents, a large portion of whom were students in high school and college. At some point the idea of a traffic safety advisory committee was hatched. The thought was for forming a citizens committee to work with police and public works on traffic safety issues; the focus would be on education, engineering, and enforcement; the product would be advice to the Town Council for programs that should be pursued. The Town Council liked the concept, and a charter was developed for what was called TSAC, the Traffic Safety Advisory Committee.

Citizens were invited to apply for appointment to TSAC. A number volunteered and several were selected. The first public meeting heard several minor safety issues, some of which came directly from the public. One of the first requests came from a citizen who demanded that Rheem Blvd., one of the town's arterial roadways, be blocked-off at the intersection with St. Mary's Road. The citizen—we'll call him the Tank—forcefully argued that traffic on Rheem Blvd., in a stretch that passes through a dense neighborhood, had become unsafe on account of speeders. The solution—in his view, the only solution— was simply to prohibit vehicles from reaching St. Mary's Road. However, the arterial was important for good traffic circulation in the vicinity of St. Mary's College, and blocking the road made no sense. The Tank wasn't one bit polite advancing his demand. He must have thought intimidation would be effective with TSAC, but he failed to appreciate that the police department's TSAC representative—a sergeant on the police force—didn't appreciate being threatened. She sternly invited the Tank to behave. He did, and the proposal went nowhere.

TSAC had heard the proposal for the speed bumps when it was originally brought to the committee by the town engineer. It was TSAC who advised that speed bumps would be a wise safety feature from a traffic calming standpoint, and that they should be "slightly raised." Subsequently, when much larger speed bumps were constructed, TSAC suggested the speed bumps be reduced in size. But by then, the speed bump issue had acquired a life of its own and had become a matter of bitter local politics.

TSAC's focus was on townwide traffic calming. In 2007, there were three traffic fatalities in Lamorinda, all related to speeding vehicles. This caused widespread alarm, and the citizens of the three Lamorinda jurisdictions encouraged their councils to do something about it. This public outpouring inspired the Slow Down Lamorinda! campaign, which was launched at the beginning of the summer when schools were out. The program was highly publicized and featured saturation of the three communities with police enforcement. Things did improve a bit . . . for a while.[9]

Lamorinda "virtual" police force: representatives from, at left, Orinda; center, Moraga; and, at right, Lafayette, united in a combined working relationship, 2007. (Town of Moraga)

For several years, Lafayette had been attempting to slow traffic and had met with some success. One of their more impressive tools was a guide for traffic calming, which discussed proven methods. The emphasis was on education, enforcement, and engineering methods. This seemed appropriate for Moraga, so I, as TSAC chair, decided to propose adapting it to Moraga's needs. The committee concurred with my suggestion, and I set out to rewrite the Lafayette guide as Moraga's traffic calming bible. Why did I take this on? Because I like doing that kind of thing—I suppose it's the Yes Person in me.

Public reaction was not positive. Several individuals challenged whether such a guide was necessary at all. Another citizen, who had recently joined TSAC—replacing an original TSAC member who had left the committee—rejected the new guide entirely. He was a Know-It-All who asserted that Moraga should write a completely different guide. So, a TSAC subcommittee was formed with the Know-It-All as chair to write something new.

Months later, a new guide was finally produced, which accomplished little more than the first guide. It just looked different. At that point, it dawned on me what had happened. What was important to those who didn't like the guide I had written was that it wasn't theirs. They wanted the guide to be their own. I should have kept my fingers off the keys and let others do the work. It would have avoided some of the angst that was experienced.

In a few years, several new individuals joined the Town Council who didn't share the view that Moraga had a traffic calming need. In their opinion traffic calming was invasive and unnecessary for a town like ours. A motion was made to dissolve TSAC entirely, which narrowly passed.

So, much for good intentions . . . TSAC didn't fly.

Hacienda de las Flores: A Failure to Cooperate

When the Hacienda de las Flores was purchased by the town, it was intended to be a public park, with recreation programs for citizen enjoyment its primary purpose. Soon, the lovely ambience of the place suggested it also would be popular as a venue for weddings and other large events. So, the Hacienda became just that, a place many couples chose as the location for their wedding. The town moved into the role of wedding planners and producers of many events every year. While revenues from these events were significant, they were insufficient to cover maintenance costs, much less to make any significant capital improvements. The town kept on losing money, and the property gradually deteriorated.

Moraga citizens who loved the Hacienda responded as best they could. The Hacienda Foundation was established to try to increase public awareness of the venue, and to encourage increased public usage. The Foundation sponsored numerous maintenance and improvement projects. Local service clubs got involved. One project by the local Kiwanis Club repainted all the first-floor rooms and made improvements to the restrooms. Another project refurbished the kitchen. And another thoroughly cleaned and repainted the interior of the pavilion and remodeled the restrooms. Events like Cinco de Mayo and Oktoberfest were held annually as fundraisers and to improve public awareness of the Hacienda.

Hacienda de las Flores, wedding reception, ca. 2015. (Photo: Town of Moraga)

While all these efforts contributed to the upkeep of the grand old property and provided wonderful opportunities for public enjoyment, the town continued to suffer financially. Moreover, increased competition from other venues in the immediate area eroded the Hacienda's market position as a wedding venue. A $250,000 annual general expense persistently weighed on the town's financial health, and the drain on limited town staff clearly was not sustainable. Something had to be done.

The basic problem was that the Hacienda property was underutilized. More could be done with the property, but any major improvements would require significant planning involving broad public participation and a substantial infusion of funds. Beginning in 2006, the Hacienda Foundation conducted strategic planning exercises intended to provide a road map for how to make the property a financially viable enterprise. However, there didn't appear to be any prospect of coalescing around ideas that had broad public appeal. The Foundation's efforts seemed for naught.

A commonly heard new idea for use for the Hacienda was as a dining establishment. The upshot of this interest came in early 2014 when the town manager suggested that a small restaurant operation be established at Hacienda to test whether there would be demand for such a business. A local restauranteur, who was looking for a new place of business, came to an agreement with the town to establish a breakfast and lunch operation using the premises in their current conditions. Moragans loved Café Hacienda; some diners came from out of town to enjoy their meals. This six-month trial indicated that a properly-run restaurant could be a successful venture.

Then, when the Joint Facilities Planning Subcommittee was considering the town's recreation needs and needed facilities, the idea of converting the Hacienda into a community center received much attention. The conclusion of the subcommittee's study was that the town should consider engaging professional services to assess new opportunities for the Hacienda. (See details of the Joint Facilities Planning in Chapter 6.)

In 2015, the town manager suggested that professional talent be engaged to help with "a process that could completely change the property from a charming but often sleeping beauty into a vibrant world-class destination."[10] An entrepreneurial citizen had suggested that a few top architectural firms be asked to study different uses of the property through a public-private partnership. He recommended transforming the town property by possibly adding a boutique hotel or a restaurant, or perhaps a wine storing and tasting facility, as well as preserving some of the land for public use. The Town Council liked the idea, and, encouraged by the trial restaurant's success, authorized the town manager to engage a suitable architectural firm. After competitive proposal bidding, an excellent architect was selected.

In June 2015, a seven-month study was commenced; it involved community meetings, discussions with major stakeholder groups (Hacienda Foundation, Lamorinda Wine Growers, St. Mary's College, and the Town Council), local restauranteurs, and developers in the field of entertainment and hospitality. Community meetings were conducted as interactive workshops, which provided opportunities for the public to voice their views on Hacienda uses. The architect conducted several meetings with town departments and the fire district to understand the physical and operational constraints of the Hacienda property. Design work then proceeded.

Two concepts were offered:

Concept A—A community conference center and inn

Concept B—A community arts park, which would forego any restaurant or lodging

Concept A was considerably more expensive ($22 million) than Concept B ($12 million). But the architect offered a phased approach to Concept A: The conference center would include a restaurant, bar, garden banquet room, and several meeting rooms; the small inn would have five guest rooms, and be a good start that could lead to eventual expansion of adding eighteen small cottages, a wine cave and tasting facility, and major renovations to the pavilion, including a new pool and bathhouse. This approach would allow adjusting for market conditions as they became better understood, and would have an initial investment that would approach about $6.3 million.[11]

The phased plan was endorsed by the Town Council and put before the public in February 2016. While many liked the plan, there was a loud protest from some public figures who had earned reputations for not liking anything the Town Council proposed. This exceeded mere sniping; the attacks against the plan were frontal and vehement. Allegations were shouted about nefarious motives of some council members (including myself). And, strangely, some new protests surfaced that focused on the margins of the proposal. One such misconception was regarding demand for the hotel services of the inn. The claim was that Moraga could not support such accommodations, but it was pointed out that St. Mary's College alone would likely occupy the inn almost all of the time. The argument raged on. It wasn't a happy outcome, and the proposal went into limbo.

In April 2016, with no funding available to continue the architect's study, the Town Council established a Hacienda Subcommittee to study further potential Hacienda uses and explore the restaurant concept more carefully.[12] The subcommittee identified a restaurant operator who was looking for a new place of business, and they fashioned a deal with him. However, by the time the Moraga attorneys had completed the lease agreement in May 2018, the restaurant operator realized that the town's liability and capital improvement demands were unacceptably onerous. He backed out.

Over the next few years, the Hacienda Subcommittee searched for firms who might be interested in operations at Hacienda under a public-private partnership arrangement. After several disappointments, Wedgewood Weddings submitted a proposal to manage

Hacienda event operations. The Town Council heard the proposal to execute a lease with Wedgewood for exclusive rights to conduct major events on the property, effective November 2021. Wedgewood was awarded those rights.[13]

What happened? While the quality of the architect's work was high, the process was robust, and the recommendations were fundamentally sound, the public never fully embraced what was proposed. Part of the reason was that during the time the architect's report was being prepared, the process became rushed. By the time the report draft went public, it seemed overwhelming to many people. The Hacienda project was transformative and obviously very expensive. But it was too much to swallow. The public simply would not accept it, even when the project was configured in phases. What was missing was the kind of outreach that had been done for the Measure K campaign. Had such an effort been undertaken, and done carefully and without rushing, the project might have gained altitude and been approved. But such wasn't the case here, and the project that had been proposed by the consultant failed.

Why did it have to fail? Part of the reason was due to the town staff's approach to dealing with the public. The Parks and Recreation director at the time was a well-liked and hard-working individual, who relied on the consultants he managed. By his nature he always wanted to please others. However, he was constrained in this instance by an insufficient budget to do the feasibility studies as thoroughly as they needed to be done—especially the hotel marketing part of the program. When challenged in public, he found it necessary to suggest that the study was incomplete. This unfairly undermined the entire project and undermined the Parks and Recreation director's credibility.

Furthermore, the director was inclined to push ahead when it was evident that the public was not ready. He resisted the notion of extensive public outreach since this would have drawn out the study process by many months. (In the case of Measure K, the outreach process had taken over a year!) The result was that the public didn't fully understand the proposed plan. They resisted the message, which prompted their adverse reactions.

Other factors were the struggles between the Town Council, town staff, and the Hacienda Foundation. The Foundation believed the Hacienda's future was their domain; the Town Council thought otherwise; and the town staff just wanted to get things done. There was little meeting of the minds, and the result was the town's proposed plan was not supported by the very ones whose support was essential. The same kind of struggle was in play with the Moraga Chamber of Commerce. It seemed each organization thought they were running the show. In the end, the show simply failed.

As was once said,

You can accomplish anything if you're willing to
let someone else take the credit.[14] —*Tip O'Neill*

Triathlon: A Terrific Yet Unsustainable Event

For years, the town has held the annual Pear & Wine Festival in celebration of the town's agricultural heritage—namely, pear production. The daylong event is held at Moraga Commons. At the 2006 event, I was visiting folks on the hill that faces the band shell; I was accompanied by the Parks and Recreation director. Just then, we encountered an old friend of mine, a person deeply involved in the sports scene in Moraga. She mentioned that it would be great if the town could organize a triathlon event that could draw people from the Bay Area to Moraga for a morning of fun competition. She thought Moraga was the perfect place for such an event: Campolindo High School has a huge competition pool suitable for the 400-meter lap swim; the roads out to Canyon and Rancho Laguna Park would provide a scenic 14-mile bicycle route; and the steep hills behind Campolindo High School would provide a challenging 3-mile run for the most accomplished road runners. The event could finish with a lap on the track at Campolindo Stadium. The Parks and Recreation director, a person of amazing energy, thought this was a splendid idea, and I encouraged her to run with it. Thus was born the Moraga Treeline Triathlon.

The inaugural triathlon was held in April 2007, with some 260 entries registered. There were open men and women's divisions, and age group divisions for males and females. Anyone who applied was allowed. There was even a team representing the City of Lafayette—the mayor, city manager, and a city council member—who completed the course in respectable time. Numerous athletes with special needs competed with vigor. A huge group of volunteers turned out to help with competition management, traffic control, and the many logistical details that such an event entailed. The bright spring day was glorious, and fun was had by athletes and volunteers alike. Revenues covered expenses, and the net proceeds were dedicated to the town's CERT program (Citizen Emergency Response Team).[15]

The Parks and Recreation director moved on to another city, and she was replaced by another enthusiastic director—one who intended to make the triathlon even more grand. By 2011, the event drew 372 entries, and the volunteers came out in droves. The racecourse was festive with large crowds cheering on the athletes as they whizzed by on their bicycles. A bagpiper from Canyon was posted at Canyon Road and Camino Pablo; he piped encouragement to every cyclist who passed by. His rendition of "Chariots of Fire" was especially memorable. The joy for the athletes and spectators was something to behold.[16]

But as with his predecessor, the enthusiastic Parks and Recreation director left for another city, and he was replaced with a person who didn't share his special love for the triathlon. By that time, it was clear that the event was a major drain on the town staff for organizing and staging the event, the magnitude of which had grown so much that professional services had to be engaged to handle the technical side of the event. This assistance eroded the net proceeds that had been earned in former years. Moreover, the number of town staff and volunteers that had been quite large was not sustainable. The new Parks and Recreation director might have signaled the town manager, who was also new to Moraga, that the event was not something that should be continued. Then geotechnical problems at the Canyon Road bridge caused the bridge to be condemned and require replacement. This cut the road to Canyon, which meant no more triathlon bicycle route for about two years. The last Moraga Treeline Triathlon was held in 2017. Then in 2020, the COVID-19 epidemic developed, which prohibited any crowd-gatherings such as a triathlon.

While it was disappointing that this community event would not be continued, the reasons for not doing so were clear and understandable. Ten years wasn't a bad run for an event that had brought so much joy to so many.

Storm Drain Fee: Half-Baked Plans Never Sell

An important part of the Revenue Enhancement Committee's focus was the town's storm drain system.[17] Certainly the roads that convey traffic and the drainage system that conveys storm water are both paramount. But given chronic limitations on annual budgets for infrastructure maintenance, roadways took precedence. This is why attention on Measure K was focused on pavement rehabilitation. Storm drains would have to be treated on a case-by-case basis.

Storm Drain Master Plan

The town's storm drain system comprises some 30 miles of drainage pipes and about 2,500 feet of culverts. Approximately 41 percent of the system was built prior to 1964. Drainage pipes were made of various materials, depending on the technologies of the time: corrugated metal pipe (CMP), reinforced concrete pipe (RCP), clay pipe, and plastics. In 1965 alone, 35,000 feet of new pipes were installed, about 30,000 feet of which were less than 40" diameter; the rest were very large pipes up to 96" diameter. As of 2009, about 90 percent of the town's system drainage pipe was less than 40" diameter.

The town's storm drain system does not include privately owned storm drainage pipes and culverts, of which there are many. All the drainage facilities beneath the two shopping centers are privately owned, and most of these—built in the 1970s—are large diameter CMP as large as 96" diameter. Based on industry average expected life expectancy of sixty years, one would expect that by 2010, these large-diameter pipes could be about forty years old and likely would require attention by their owners. Given that many of the pipes elsewhere in the town were built in the 1955-65 timeframe, a lot of those early pipes would be well on their way to needing serious work, possibly replacement. In short, storm drains were a problem that could not be deferred any longer.

The town had completed video surveys of larger pipes (36" and up), which showed that deterioration of many of them was advanced. Failed larger pipes would not only be much more expensive to repair or replace than smaller pipes, but their failure could potentially be much more disruptive, especially in the shopping centers where business would be adversely impacted. Indeed, exactly that happened in January 2006, when a segment of the 96" pipe beneath Rheem Blvd. at the entrance to the Rheem Shopping Center collapsed, opening a large sinkhole. That failure served as a wakeup-call warning of other potentially disruptive events.

The Revenue Enhancement Committee had recommended that the town establish a $20 million remedial work program spread over a thirty-year period, meaning an annual expenditure of about $670,000. The town's problem was simply that such a program would compete for pavement projects. While Measure K authorized a General Tax, which could be used for any purposes the Town Council directed, it was recognized that, as a matter of honoring commitments to the public, Measure K money would go toward pavements and nothing else. This made funding nonpavement projects a political issue, not a legal one. As long as I was on the Town Council, I strongly advised my colleagues not to use Measure K funds for anything except roads, unless there was a clear connection between a storm drainage problem and a road that needed repair. That thinking held sway during the first five years of Measure K funding. Pavement conditions throughout town dramatically improved, but very little was spent on storm drainage.

Rheem Shopping Center

Down Under

Completed Repair Patch on Rheem Blvd.

Collapsed 96" storm drain under Rheem Blvd., January 2006. (Photos: Town of Moraga)

Nonetheless, a master plan for storm drainage was developed as a first step of a remedial work program. The town engaged an engineering firm with expertise in citywide drainage planning to thoroughly examine the existing storm drainage system and formulate a plan for specific remedial projects. The idea was to produce a multipurpose resource guide for the town's annual stormwater improvement planning.

The consultant required over a year to complete the field investigations and perform the analyses of the townwide drainage system. The final report in July 2015 pointed out that most projects in the $26 million program were related to the capacity of pipes and creek culverts; a small portion was related to pipe conditions, streets, and other minor issues. One third of the projects were rated High priority, about 40 percent Moderate, and the rest Low priority. As a general assessment, the report noted that:

> . . . although the majority of the pipes are in good condition, some of the pipes would benefit from maintenance to remove debris. . . . In addition to the identified improvement projects, it is recommended the town set aside an annual budget of $240,000 to televise, clean, and replace/repair any pipes that are found to be in poor condition. Pipes should be televised under the streets to be repaired in the following year to coordinate pavement repair and storm drain repairs.[18]

The master plan was an important element in the annual planning for improvements to the storm drain system. Accordingly, attention was directed to implementing the consultant's advice.

Deliver Us from Sinkholes

Nearly a year later in March, 2016, the town was hit by a huge storm that dumped massive amounts of rainwater over a period of nearly two weeks. On Sunday, March 13, the pavement of Rheem Blvd. and the adjacent sidewalk at the intersection with Center Street started to collapse into a sinkhole that rapidly opened, swallowing a traffic light and an electrical switch apparatus. The sinkhole was 15 feet wide by 20 feet long by 15 feet deep. As debris fell into the sinkhole, a 4-inch-high pressure gas line ruptured, which prompted the evacuation of businesses adjacent to the collapsed sidewalk. At the time, the nearby Rheem Theater was showing a matinee at which some 100 children were attending. The children were ordered to shelter in place. The town activated the Emergency Operations Center, and Pacific Gas and Electric workers quickly shut down the gas supply for some 2,600 Moraga households. The concern was that the ruptured gas line could turn into a disaster much like the San Bruno gas pipeline explosion in 2010, which claimed eight lives.[19]

On March 16, 2016, the town declared a State of Emergency. Meanwhile, many of the businesses in the immediate vicinity were forced to close temporarily, owing to concern for further incidents and disruption to vehicle and foot traffic in the area. Soon thereafter, the town engaged in an extensive forensic study of the incident to determine what had happened. According to the town engineer, a section of the 96-inch CMP downstream of the same pipe that failed ten years earlier, had failed for the same reasons.

Two months later, the town was able to reopen Rheem Blvd. to circumvent the sinkhole repair project.[20]

Shortly after the sinkhole developed, the town was hosting the Contra Costa Mayors' Conference at St. Mary's College. As mayor at the time, I was acting as host to mayors and council members from the eighteen cities of Contra Costa County, plus numerous county and special agency officials. As part of the festivities, I had arranged that an invocation be delivered by Brother Mel Anderson, a longtime member of the St. Mary's College and Town of Moraga communities. Brother Mel, who stood about 6'5", rose and cried out in stentorian voice a supplication heard throughout the crowded hall:

O Lord! Deliver us from sinkholes!

No more fitting a prayer could have been offered.

Storm Drain Fee Controversy

The March 2016 sinkhole compelled the Town Council to think with urgency about how the program outlined in the 2015 Storm Drain Master Plan could be implemented. If the 2005 sinkhole had been a wakeup call and the Master Plan had sounded a warning, then the 2016 sinkhole should have convinced any serious citizen that storm drainage remedial work warranted a much higher priority. In my last year on the Town Council, and as sitting mayor, I made it my top priority to find a revenue source to fund the rehabilitation and maintenance program that had been outlined in the master plan.

The community outreach experience and Measure K served as the basis for thinking through how to deliver a long-term funding source for the long-term challenge of rehabilitation and maintenance of the town's storm drains. But the effort leading to Measure K success was lengthy—nearly two years—and no one could honestly believe that the storm drain situation had not already reached crisis proportions. So the Town Engineer set out to develop a strategy for moving forward on an expedited basis.

The engineering planning was sufficiently developed to determine a funding method. Of all the approaches considered from the time the Revenue Enhancement Committee had surveyed the field of potential funding sources, a property-related assessment fee made the most sense. The question then was whether a property-related fee for storm drainage purposes required a so-called "protest ballot" process. On the advice of one of the citizens who had been an important contributor to the Measure K funding decisions, such an election would be prudent. Therefore, the protest ballot process was put into motion.[21]

Under California State Law, a property-related fee must be levied on property according to each property's contribution to the service being provided. This requires that every water-shedding structure and surface be accounted for, including those of schools, churches, and municipal buildings. No surface is exempted; it doesn't matter what uses the buildings serve. Everything and everyone are included.

A campaign committee was formed with several of the same individuals who had served on the Yes on Measure K committee. The usual paraphernalia was prepared that explained the fee and encouraged citizens to vote for it. The campaign was dubbed Save Our Stormdrains (SOS). Pamphlets were prepared and distributed by volunteers who walked the streets, leaving them at doors. A speaker's bureau was established for coordinating visits by SOS volunteers to conduct informational meetings in people's homes. Letters to The Editor of the local newspaper were written and published over the month preceding the May 8, 2018 election.

The opposition to the storm drain fee was loud and persistent. The Snipers commenced firing, and the Know-It-Alls clung to the notion that Moraga was a profligate spender, spending money with abandon. The Whiners complained that schools would be required to pay the fee, which would—in their view—never, ever, be acceptable. It also was unacceptable that there was no sunset to the fee—that, instead, the fee would be in force indefinitely unless rescinded by the Town Council. Senior citizens would be required to pay just like everyone else; this was unheard of, since all ballot measures floated by the schools always offered an opt-out provision for seniors. Another group of Know-It-Alls complained there was no explicit financing in place for the program over the initial years. In their opinion, this was another example of irresponsible town governance. Finally, many opponents refused to understand the protest ballot process; some of them were suspicious that something nefarious was going on. So they rejected it entirely.

In April, a month before the election, the local newspaper conducted parallel interviews of proponents of the storm drain fee and opponents of the fee. The same questions were posed, and responses were reported in the paper. The opponents called themselves "SmartMoraga" (SM). The SM people denied there was any emergency warranting a storm drain fee; after all, the town's consultant had opined that "the overall condition of the storm drain system in Moraga is very good." They maintained that the town had not saved anything for storm drain work, which they viewed simply as mismanagement. They insisted that Moraga already had sufficient funds to do whatever work needed to be done, and that any fees collected would be double-dipping. They maintained that the town had no plan and didn't know what it was doing. They criticized the imposition of the storm drain fee on schools, churches, and even on other government agencies, ignoring that to exempt these entities would be a violation of State Law. They insisted that the town should start saving by spending on "needs" and not on "wants."

The interview served to demonstrate an opposition that was not interested in the reasons behind the fee and offered no information that was helpful. SmartMoraga no doubt confused, more than helped, voters who were trying to understand what was being discussed. They behaved like classic Think-They-Know-It-Alls. However, they did succeed in confusing the conversation about the storm drain fee to the point where a lot of voters just said no. This very well might have been their strategy.[22]

In aggregate, there were a lot of negativities surrounding the fee proposal. While it had concerned some of us on the SOS committee that the protest votes might defeat the fee, many other members were convinced that the fee made so much sense that it would sail to victory. Such wasn't the case: The storm drain fee failed to win a majority of Yes votes (of 5,381 ballots cast, the "Yes" votes were only 47.96 percent of the total).[23]

Why did this happen? Several factors seem important:

First, the major landowner in town was entitled to cast over 200 ballots. Knowing that landowner's attitudes toward anything the town wanted to do, it's not unreasonable to conclude that that single landowner might have been the major reason the measure did not win those votes, which were far more than the 137 votes by which the measure failed.

Second, while it had become clear to many people that storm drains represented a major problem for Moraga, it was the second sinkhole that pushed the town to pursue vigorously for a storm drain fee. Considerable energy developed surrounding the fee, as Town Council members and senior staff made it increasingly clear that a storm drain fee was essential. Engineering staff unquestionably understood the technical problems, and they sensed the political urgency swelling about them. So the staff rushed the process, curtailing the extensive outreach progress that had been successful for Measure K. Many questions posed by the public went unanswered, or they were answered only in perfunctory ways. When it came time to vote, many voters still had questions. As is human nature, when someone is asked to decide on something not entirely understood, that person is more likely to vote No.

Third—and this is also a consequence of the process being rushed—a detailed program and financing needs for the initial several years had not been thoroughly developed. Too many voters concluded that the town didn't really know what needed to be done and in what order. This led many to view the entire program as bogus, which was an unfortunate conclusion.

Last, the storm drain fee was a culmination of several years of episodes in which the public was at odds with the Town Council. It started with the Speed Bump fiasco and then the Dog Park controversy. Moreover, there remained a lot of people who simply did not believe the town's financial position was as dire as they'd been telling them. Too many residents didn't believe the Revenue Enhancement Committee's findings; they rejected RECON as propaganda; they were convinced the town was being incompetently run and could not be trusted with the revenues that they imagined would be realized by the storm drain fee. It didn't help that the local newspaper had hired a staff writer who, for most of 2017, couldn't seem to write anything but disparaging things about the state of town governance.[24]

One "Letter to The Editor" contributor expressed herself plainly and succinctly in support of the storm drain fee and discouraged any vote against it:

> Some have suggested voting against the Fee to "send a message to the Town Council"; it would be a mistake to protest the fee program to voice dissatisfaction with past or present Town Council. We cannot afford to kick this can farther down the road; if you would like to change our local representatives, you can do so in November 2018 and November 2020 [when there are elections for open Council seats].[25]

Indeed, that's what happened. The mayor, who was up for re-election, was voted out. As for me, I had decided long before (in November 2015) that it was time to retire from local politics. I might have been cast out as well. Once again, it had been made quite clear that . . . All Politics Is Local.

Storm Drain Postscript

Even though I was no longer involved in an official capacity after the December 2016 general election, it's worth mentioning that the story didn't end with my departure. During March 2019, heavy rains continued their attack of Moraga's decrepit drainage pipes under the Rheem Shopping Center. Land movement under the pavement at the service station at the intersection of Rheem Blvd. and Center St. caused a new sinkhole. Service station pavement damage was 10' long by 3' wide, while the actual sinkhole was 5' by 2'. This new sinkhole was about 75 feet across Rheem Blvd. from the 2016 sinkhole, and directly over the 96-inch pipe that had been involved in that failure. The town's immediate concern was that this new development might be a harbinger of worse things to come in the vicinity. A video inspection of the pipe determined that immediate attention was necessary. Since the pipe was on private property, responsibility was with the property owner. He did not share the town's view, and the legal problems went on from there.

The second item of importance after my time on the Town Council was the so-called "Amazon tax." When the Measure K financing plan was in the process of being developed in 2012, the town's sales and use tax applied only to purchases of goods purchased in Moraga (plus automobiles, boats, and airplanes purchased anywhere else). The 1 percent tax authorized by Measure K earned the town about $1 million annually. However, State Law changed in 2019 requiring that so-called "marketplace facilitators" like Amazon would be responsible for collecting the sales tax on goods they sold for delivery into California.[26] This nearly doubled Moraga's Measure K sales tax revenues. Not only could Moraga's pavement repair program be more aggressive, but more storm drainage work could be funded—a fortunate windfall that made up for the disappointing failure of the storm drain fee.

CHAPTER 8

Reflections

RECOUNTING EIGHTEEN YEARS OF PUBLIC SERVICE hasn't been a casual meandering down Memory Lane. Reconstructing things can be difficult and sometimes painful. Honest appraisal has required some humility, for not everything was rosy. While much was, some was not. Readers should be assured that this one-time public servant didn't always have such a swell time, even though much of the experience was satisfying and left me feeling good about my contributions. More important, however, are some of the most significant lessons that I learned—and in some cases relearned—as the years moved on. It's these that I wish to share. Others might appreciate them in the context of their own situations.

This chapter is about reflections. The previous chapters have talked a bit about me to introduce readers to the fellow who was trying to have a positive impact. The Town of Moraga is introduced in summary fashion. When writing this book, I realized there was much I didn't know about my own town, and I suspect I'm not alone in this ignorance. I came to appreciate the history of the town, which tells me much about the people who have lived there and why they acted as they did . . . and still do. Their values became clear, which helps explain what motivates them and drives their behavior. As is always the case, some of the people with whom a local politician has to deal are difficult folks. They behave in ways that might seem strange to some. Certainly, they can be annoying, and their behavior patterns are quite predictable. Yet they must be dealt with, and delicately so. They are, after all, voters who can mean success or failure of something a town official wants to do. After all, politics is the art of persuasion . . . and alienating someone isn't the most effective way to win someone over.

The meat of the story has been the case studies of those major things that went well and those that did not during my tenure. I know a lot more about every one of these cases than most anyone else, yet I appreciate that most readers don't want too many details.

Subsequently, I have treated each case in summary form, focusing on what went well, or didn't. Many of the anecdotes speak of the behavior of some of the difficult people. That's important because it's those people, and how I handled (or mishandled) them, that had a lot of bearing on the success or failure of any issue. I found that revisiting some of these topics was difficult, yet largely refreshing, because they say a lot about what it's like to try and accomplish things in a place where all politics is local.

I began this story by introducing Tip O'Neill, the sage New England politician whom I knew by reputation when I was a boy in Boston. Old Tip was a remarkable fellow, not so much for what he did but for how he did it. He had incredible street smarts, and an uncommon appreciation of his fellow man. He liked just about everyone, even his political foes. They liked him, and he was enormously respected. His simple words of wisdom pierced my adolescent arrogance, and I've never forgotten them. Tip's important thoughts made lasting impressions, and many of his nuggets have stayed with me. They shine in the book you're reading. He hit the nail on the head more than I ever could, no matter how hard I tried. As you no doubt have realized by now, I believe that his most unforgettable nugget is the aphorism . . . All Politics Is Local.

Old Tip leaves me with at least ten impressions, all of which have emerged in this story. At the risk of this appearing like a check list of how one should behave in the political arena, I'll address each one that I think is important:

Never Forget Those Who Matter

A successful figure in local politics is one who never forgets those who matter. It starts with the voters who put the politician in office. They might like you, but don't ever think they worship you. They'll watch your every move and are happy to throw mud and brickbats at you when they don't like something you've done. But if you deliver on what you said you'd do, they'll probably appreciate you, possibly respect you. They might even re-elect you.

It's a good idea to seek out those who are influential. In a small town like Moraga, there are a few of these folks who have earned reputations that entitle them to opine on things in public and enjoy an attentive audience. If these influential people appreciate you and the things you are trying to do, chances are good they will talk about you to others. Your stature can be elevated and the chances for advancing your ideas will be enhanced. This is not to suggest you ought to "suck up" to an influencer. Most of them got where they are largely by recognizing phonies. Being genuine is the best approach.

It's good to seek out people who want to help. Engage those who appear to have genuine interest in what you want to accomplish. Willing and even busy people invariably like to be asked to join and pitch in. Invite them to join and to participate. They all can contribute and likely will if asked, and when they become involved in what you are doing, they're likely to support you faithfully. They like to be acknowledged, no matter how insignificant their contributions might be, no matter who they are. They might be a volunteer, a friend, or perhaps a staff person working for the town . . . it doesn't matter. Always thank the on-duty police officer you encounter on Thanksgiving Day for being of service to the town on a holiday when most other people are with family and friends. Know who packs your parachute.[1]

I think it's best to ignore the perennial Snipers. These people are attention seekers at your expense. They usually have nothing worthwhile to contribute and they aren't interested in helping you succeed. Their performance is on display for all to see, and generally, they say more about themselves than about you or anyone else. If confronted with a suggestion that they participate and help, they will often claim they are too busy with other pursuits; they haven't the time to actually help out. More often than not, they aren't worth taking seriously.[2]

Focus on Local Matters, Leave the Rest to Others

Local politicians should stay close to home, focusing on local matters that concern citizens of the town where you live and where you were elected to serve. While it can be tempting to become involved in wider issues, at the county or state level, it can be dangerous since attention can be diverted to things that aren't priorities for your fellow neighbors. I can recall a wandering politician in a Contra Costa city who was enamored by her popularity on the statewide circuit (League of California Cities). She campaigned hard and was elected to a high position on the League Board of Directors. It's not certain what she accomplished in her statewide position, but she certainly didn't attend to pressing matters at home. A scandal erupted in her city in which she was implicated, yet she seemed too preoccupied by statewide business to manage it. She was voted out of office at the next election.

Council members are obliged to accept positions on committees and boards beyond the borders of the town. It's part of the job. Many of these positions have relevance to important issues with the town, but many do not. Where something has a direct bearing on town business, it deserves attention; otherwise, leave the matter to others. There's enough to do at home without being unnecessarily distracted by extraneous issues. Let someone else knock themselves out.

The local politician who is perceived as genuinely pursuing the voters' interests is the one who is likely to be appreciated and respected . . . and re-elected. Serving the voters is always top priority. Straying off the reservation might be tempting, and possibly personally rewarding, even though it might have no bearing on your official job. It's always important to keep in mind the distinction between wanting to do the job as opposed to wanting to have the job.

Trying to Do Too Much Too Quickly Never Works

Tip O'Neill relates, "The temptation, particularly for a new president, is to try and get it done too much too soon." He was referring to Jimmy Carter who, upon entering the presidency, attacked all sorts of things right away. "He had too many balls in the air at the same time. He dropped a few and never fully recovered. Ronald Reagan was more focused on one thing, his economic plan, and [he] succeeded. . . ."[3] O'Neill could have been talking about me—the Moraga firebrand—who, upon election to the Town Council, went after everything that crossed my mind, and expected that everyone would follow. This never works, partly because too many balls start flying and being a juggler is not everyone's strong suit. It clearly wasn't mine. Rather than aggressively attacking Moraga's traffic calming subject as I did, I would have been better off working through the local politics before plunging into what was a swamp.

Even by the time I was into my third term, I was still allowing myself to try and move more aggressively than was wise. I was brutally reminded that most citizens don't like to have things pushed down their throat. Dealing with an important asset like Moraga's Hacienda de las Flores aroused special interest for many of the town's citizens. They needed to absorb what was being proposed. They needed to digest what was thrown at them, to discuss it, argue about it, consider adjustments, and then decide. O'Neill draws a parallel when he advises: ". . . trust the system. The Constitution gave the representatives the right to deliberate[,] and they just want to exercise it."[4] Same for the people of Moraga. Neither an over-energetic Town Council member nor an impatient town staffer can change that. Nothing can be rushed. Be patient and never lose faith that something good can happen . . . in good time.

Do No Harm

I received a bit of important advice when I was first elected to the Town Council. If you can't honestly see that something you want to do is going to help people and improve things, don't do it; if something isn't serving a legitimate public purpose, don't touch it. Above all, do no harm.[5]

Sometimes the urge to jump into an issue overcomes better judgment. This is what happened with the speed bump fiasco described in the preceding chapter; the urge to impose traffic calming measures clouded my judgment, as I realized when convincing information had been received from the Fire District that the speed bumps were a mistake from the standpoint of degraded emergency response. The potential for harm was there. It was time to stop and get it right.

Admit Mistakes, Early and Often

Making mistakes is bound to happen. Otherwise, you probably aren't trying to do much. Mistakes go hand in hand with progress. But what's unacceptable is not realizing a mistake has been made when new evidence clearly demonstrates an error, and then not admitting it. As painful as admissions of culpability can sometimes be, not coming clean is inexcusable. New information should be considered seriously; new facts and circumstances must be completely understood; and then, perhaps, a prior decision should be rescinded. No time to dawdle, no time to be wishy-washy. Decide and take corrective action.

Public admission is a powerful thing. There's nothing wrong with a sincere mea culpa. Particularly in the Dog Park controversy, I found it important to ensure that the local press understood my side of the story, and that the press was willing to be honest in their reporting. The value of a friendly press can't be over-emphasized. However, I would caution that such moments of humility should not be viewed as opportunities to grab headlines.

I was pleasantly surprised when seeking re-election in 2008 (after the speed bump fiasco) to hear from a few influential voters that they appreciated my honesty in admitting my errors and trying to make things right. People notice these things, and they usually admire a bit of humility.

Celebrate Success
Praise publicly . . . and do so often.

Credit others foremost. It's been said earlier in this story, much can get done if it doesn't matter who gets the credit. Wasting time and goodwill squabbling over territorial rights on an issue is a sure way to ensure that nothing good will get done. That's what happened with the Hacienda studies episode; failure to cooperate doomed this otherwise commendable project.

Reluctance to seek credit is one reason why I don't like to be in the forefront when there's a dedication of something like a new building. I much prefer to let others take the credit; they usually deserve praise every bit as much as I do. Yet I'm always willing to spend time and money on celebrations of success. There's nothing more uplifting, for instance, than having a State of The Town address that is robust in humanity and tasteful humor. Among my greatest pleasures as mayor were the three times that I delivered such addresses. Oh sure, some Snipers criticized me for being wasteful. But I focused on the joy on the faces of citizens and town staff who were present—it was something to behold. There was nothing more gratifying than to be complimented by the police chief when, after one such address, said he was proud to be part of the town. That justified it all.

Look hard for opportunities to celebrate good things. In 2008, three athletes from Campolindo High School represented the United States in the Beijing Olympics (Peter Varellas, Water Polo; Kim Vandenberg, Swimming; and Jeff Stevens, Baseball). Three Olympians from Campolindo Class of 2002 in the small Town of Moraga! That's amazing and certainly called for a celebration. So we had a huge banner made for prominent display in town. Many people were so proud, not to mention the athletes' parents who attended the Town Meeting where a proclamation that honored their sons and daughter was read.

Show Up

Another bit of advice from one of my mentors, Gayle Uilkema: Show up. The occasion doesn't matter. For a celebration of a success, you should be there, not to be in the limelight . . . just to be a part of it. Your presence means a lot to people. While I have attended too many funerals, I don't recall one that I regretted going to. Grieving parents who have lost their son in the line of duty know exactly who you are when you pass their son's casket and bow your head. They never forget your kind smile of condolence. Writing letters of condolence is not my favorite thing, but I always did it, even for someone I never knew. It's the act of kindness that means so much. People appreciate it and they respect you for it.

Be Honest

A good reputation is hard won but easily lost. It's best to foster a reputation for integrity. People recognize you for what you are, which is expressed more in what you do than in what you say. People are sensitive to your honesty as they observe you and hear what you say: Can they trust you? Are you leveling with them? Are you shooting straight? They don't like being taken for fools, so be straight with them. O'Neill advises, "In politics, I've always found that when you go out and explain your position, people will listen and respect you even if they don't agree with your point of view. Naturally, they're even more inclined to give you a fair hearing if you have a good reputation for public service."[6]

He also offers this nice bit of advice: "Tell the truth the first time so you don't have to remember what you said."[7] If you find yourself having to think hard remembering something you said, it's probably because you've said something you didn't really mean. Have a look in the mirror. What does the person looking back at you really think? Get in tune with yourself and project that to others.

And always remember: "It's a round world—what goes around, comes around."[8]

Self-Destruction and Avoiding It

The difficult people I contended with over the years brought out the best and the worst in me. Especially the Tank. Many of these people were truly annoying. Most of the time, I neither appreciated their messages nor their ways of delivering them. I strived to find ways to cope with the more difficult ones, and I had some successes. For the most part, I realized that humor was the best tonic for the venom spewed by the Tank. It got to where I would sit passively and listen to the Tank with absolutely no expression on my face. The Tank probably wasn't aware of my thoughts on his performance; he probably didn't care. What he might have realized, had he cared, is that my expressionless stare was masking a conversation I was having with myself about the idiocy of this person. One time, I imagined pushing a creme pie into the Tank's face. It helped me feel better. Usually, when the Tank was appearing to run low on shells to fire, I would simply ask if he was through, then go on to the next person. Most Tanks didn't appreciate this treatment, but what else was I to do? One thing I learned as a young boy growing up in the woods of New England, never get into a contest with a skunk; the skunk will always win, and you'll end up smelling bad. Same with the Tank: Fire back at him and the fight will be on.

One's temper can be a deadly weapon for self-destruction. Lose your temper in a public forum, and it will be a long time before people forget it. Most Moragans are civil folks and don't appreciate uncivil behavior. Better to remain silent and bite your tongue than to let forth an outburst you'll regret.

Another lesson learned early, and relearned while on the Town Council, was never to interfere with people making fools of themselves. Particularly when these people are in attack mode. Let them have their say, thank them for their contributions (even at the risk of appearing disingenuous), and move on. Invariably, they will have told everyone hearing their performances more about themselves than anything or anyone else. Let them rip!

Use of humor can be a dangerous thing. I had one colorful colleague on the Town Council who liked to tell folksy and off-color stories, often mentioning people who were known to others in the audience. While the stories were usually humorous, it was apparent that not all ears heard my colleague the way he intended. Some of his remarks, in addition to being somewhat ribald, were personally insulting if taken out of context. I was never sure he realized what he was doing. But there was no coaching him; he could fend for himself. Watching his behavior helped me double down on striving not to offend people, and to use humor only where it would not be misconstrued. I never got feedback that I was failing in that regard.

When It's Time to Quit

Many agencies impose term limits on their elected officials. For the most part there are good reasons for limits: avoiding entrenched individuals who don't bring fresh thoughts and perspectives to the table; giving others the opportunity to contribute what they can; or avoiding aged or otherwise enfeebled officeholders from hanging on to the detriment of the public good. Most Contra Costa cities do not have term limits, perhaps out of concern that there might not be a supply of fresh candidates to run for office. Moraga has never had term limits, and there has never been a council member who has been re-elected three times in succession. (At least one tried but was defeated for a fourth term.)

It seems to me that three terms are enough. Perhaps too much. The first four-year term is one for familiarization, for learning how things get done; the second can be productive; but the third is likely to be stale. I recall having a conversation with a county supervisor (Mary Nejedly Piepho) in 2015 at an event where she announced that she would not be seeking a fourth term. I asked her why, to which she responded that by the third term, you've probably done about all you can usefully do; time to let someone else have an opportunity. That resonated with my thoughts, and I thanked her for helping me decide what I was going to do. She wasn't at all surprised: "If that's what's best for you, do it." So, it was confirmed: I would not try for a fourth term.

By the time I was into my third term, I simply didn't feel the excitement of the first two terms. Part of the reason was I had experienced four town managers and we had already accomplished a lot. The failures were not pleasant, but the successes more than made up for the disappointments. The new town manager (the former police chief) would be working with a new mayor, and they could carry on as well as they could, probably better than I could have. Moreover, the incivility shown by some of the public was annoying to the point of washing away much of the joy of being a council member. It occurred to me that I just didn't want to do it anymore. The thrill had gone. So, it was time for me to go.

When you're in a public office, all you can really do is try hard by applying your best efforts. When, and if, you've done that, it's best to be grateful and move on. It's best to move out on your own terms rather than be removed by the voters.

I announced my decision not to seek re-election at the Town Council reorganization meeting in December 2012. I was relieved . . . and I never regretted it.

Are all politics really local? I think it aptly describes the politics of the Town of Moraga. Things that matter to the people of the town reflect their values and self-interests. They care about the things that affect their lives; it seems oftentimes they care about little else. Being a small town, where many people know lots of others, it doesn't take much time for a political consensus to develop around any issue—and on opposing sides of an issue. In an atmosphere where everyone has a right to say whatever comes to mind, brisk political conversation can give anything a life of its own. Getting things done in such an environment is not easy. Yet the political process must be played out. Nothing can be rushed.

Was it worth it? On balance—and I have no reservations—it was . . . At times, it was trying, to be sure, even gut-wrenching at other times. But I was in a place where I could employ my civil engineering and project management skills toward getting things done in a town where the needs were many but the resources few. A lot of good things happened that might not have had I not put my oar into the water and pulled. I was useful. Eight years down the road, I still live in Moraga, and I still have friends that I've had for years. I think most people appreciate what I did. They don't make a fuss about it. And that's just fine with me.

Endnotes

Chapter 1

1   The Kutubu Oil Development project is discussed by Jared Diamond in his book *Collapse: How Societies Choose to Fail or Succeed* (New York: Penguin Books, 2005). Professor Diamond describes how major resource extraction businesses collide with environmental interests, some with good results, others with disastrous outcomes. As an environmental consultant for the World Wildlife Fund (WWF) and a long-time monitor of Chevron's Kutubu operation in the 1990s, Diamond witnessed Chevron's Kutubu field operations during the numerous extended visits he made to the field from 1998 to 2003. Traditionally a foe of oil companies, Diamond actually lauds Chevron's environmental stewardship alongside their economic interests. He expresses his astonishment at many of the good things he witnessed, remarking at one point, "In effect, the Kutubu oil field functions as by far the largest and most rigorously controlled national park in Papua New Guinea." (See Diamond 446-52).

2   The Indonesian project envisaged a major export-oriented refinery on the island of Sumatra intended to process crude oil produced by Caltex, a joint venture of Chevron and Texaco. Called EXOR IV, the project was sponsored by Indonesian President Suharto. Political upheaval in the early 1990s led to the demise of the Suharto regime, and with it the EXOR IV project.

3   The Tengiz oil field in Kazakhstan is one of the world's largest oil fields. Located on the northeast corner of the Caspian Sea, Tengiz contains enormous oil reserves and "sour" gas (that is, the gas contains high levels of sulfur dioxide, which is a deadly gas). From the early 1990s, the Tengiz oil field has been operated by Tengizchevroil, a consortium led by Chevron. The early days of the oil field and the export pipeline through the 1990s are presented by Daniel Yergin in *The Quest* (New York: Penguin Books, 2011), 65-72. Expansion of the field after 2000 is described in "Tengiz Field," https://en.wikipedia.org/wiki/Tengiz Field, accessed Dec. 14, 2023.

4   From the outset, the Kutubu oil wells produced prodigious amounts of gas and gas liquids (butane, propane, and other light hydrocarbons). Some oil producers flare the produced gas, but neither Chevron nor the PNG government wanted to waste a valuable resource that might someday be commercialized. So the initial design called for reinjection of gas back into the oil reservoir for both gas conservation and reservoir pressure maintenance. After five years of oil production, however, the volumes of produced gas had become excessive, and Chevron wanted to export the gas and gas liquid for sale on the market. This called for a major gas export pipeline, plus marine facilities off the southern PNG coast to load gas liquids onto export tankers.

5   The gas project was sold to Exxon, who scrapped the pipeline to Australia and the gas liquids' export facilities offshore PNG. Exxon instead built the gas pipeline to carry gas from the Kutubu area to the southern coast of PNG. Exxon's pipeline was routed offshore along the southern coast of PNG to a processing plant for liquified natural gas near Port Moresby to the southeast. The LPG product was then exported to market via special LNG tankers. Exxon began operating their LNG facility in 2014. (See "PNGLNG," https://www.pnglng.com/About, accessed Dec. 15, 2023.)

6   In this instance, a church had proposed to place a large monument sign at the foot of a long access road leading to the church. There were already several directional signs elsewhere on roads within the town limits. The town's sign ordinance clearly limited the number of directional signs of any kind on town roads. The proposed monument sign would violate that limit, which was why the Planning Commission denied the proposal. Several council members thought that was wrong; several planning commissioners thought the monument sign should be allowed, but the law is the law. So the commission suggested that the council grant a variance to the ordinance and modify the ordinance to avoid such problems in the future. That was not appreciated by several council members, who instructed one of their members to have a private counseling session with me (as commission chair at the time) to point out that I should do as I was told. If I did not, I would not be reappointed to the commission at the end of my term.

7   The 2002 General Plan was not adopted by the Town Council until 2004. Disagreements over some land-use issues delayed council approval. Nonetheless, the revised plan was a considerable improvement over the 1990 General Plan. However, the goal for maintaining a minimum government was retained.

Chapter 2

1   Thomas P. (Tip) O'Neill and Gary Hymel, *All Politics Is Local and Other Rules of the Game* (Holbrook, Mass.: Bob Adams, Inc, 1994), x-xv.

2   Thomas P. O'Neill and William Novak, *The Man of the House: The Life and Political Memoirs of Speaker Tip O'Neill* (New York, St. Martin's Press, 1987).

3   It is widely believed that O'Neill coined the phrase "All Politics Is Local," employing it during a campaign in 1935. However, the phrase was used earlier by Byron Price (1891-1981), the Washington bureau chief of the Associated Press and author of the newspaper column "Politics at Random." Price wrote "politics is local" and "all politics is local politics" in February 1932, and "all politics is local in the last analysis" in July 1932. He probably coined and popularized the saying. (See Barry Popik, July 2009, https://www.barrypopik.com/ new_york_city/ entry/all_politics_is_local/, accessed Dec. 19, 2023.)

4   Tip O'Neill, *All Politics Is Local . . .*, xvi.

5   Tip O'Neill, *All Politics Is Local . . .*, 21. (In his memoir, O'Neill explains that "people like to be asked—and they like to be thanked." See Tip O'Neill, *Man of the House*, 25.)

6   Tip O'Neill, *All Politics Is Local . . .*,39-40.

7   Tip O'Neill, *All Politics Is Local . . .*, 60.

8   Tip O'Neill, *All Politics Is Local . . .*, 65.

9   Tip O'Neill, *All Politics Is Local . . .*, 71.

10   Tip O'Neill, *All Politics Is Local . . .*, 83-4.

11   Tip O'Neill, *All Politics Is Local . . .*, 174.

12   Tip O'Neill, *All Politics Is Local . . .*, 179.

13   Tip O'Neill, *All Politics Is Local . . .*, 185.

14   Tip O'Neill, *All Politics Is Local . . .*, 187-8.

15 Andrew Gelman, "All Politics Is Local? The Debate and the Graphs," see Reference 3 at https://en.wikipedia.org/wiki/All_politics_is_local, accessed Dec. 18, 2023.

16 Andrew Gelman, "All Politics Is Local? The Debate . . ."

17 Jessica Trounstine, "All Politics Is Local: The Reemergence of the Study of City Politics," *Cambridge Core, Perspective in Politics*, Cambridge University Press, Aug. 19, 2009.

18 Jessica Trounstine, 18.

19 Jessica Trounstine, 4-7.

20 The tri-city region including Lafayette, Moraga, and Orinda has been dubbed "Lamorinda" since at least the 1970s. The three cities epitomize the notion that "All Politics Is Local."

Chapter 3

1   Sandy Kimball, *Moraga's Pride: Rancho Laguna de los Palos Colorado*, 2nd ed. (1987: Moraga, Calif.: Moraga Historical Society, 2002). Moraga realtors have been known to gift a copy of this book to new homebuyers, as a gesture of welcome to this unusual community.

2   In my experiences working on various county and regional committees and commissions, I would hear comments from some representatives of cities elsewhere in the county that unmistakably suggested they considered people from the Lamorinda cities to be elitist, which in their view was not a good thing.

3   Sandy Kimball, *Moraga's Pride: . . .*, 15.

4   Sandy Kimball, *Moraga's Pride: . . .*, 43. The formal land grant was dated August 20, 1835. The Mexican government called the grant Rancho Laguna de los Palos Colorados. Gabriel Moraga, Joaquin Moraga's father, married into the Bernal family. As such, both the Moraga and Bernal families were involved as grantees in the rancho.

5   Sandy Kimball, *Moraga's Pride: . . .*, 52-9.

6   Sandy Kimball, *Moraga's Pride: . . .*, 58-61. In 1912, Horace Carpentier sold the property to James Irvine, a rancher from Southern California. It was used for some years as part of a dairy, but it was abandoned once again. Then in 1941, James Irvine's wife, Katherine, decided to rescue the Adobe. She restored and expanded it as a modern home in which she lived until she died in 1950. She willed the place to her stepson. The property was then sold to the Manuel family, and later in 1976 to the Dean Claxton family. After a century as a focal point in Moraga's history and home for numerous Moraga descendants, the Moraga Adobe became California Registered Landmark No. 509 dated 1954; in 1972, it was added to the Register of National Historic Places (Sandy Kimball, *Moraga's Pride: . . .*, 60-1). The Moraga Adobe is actually located in the City of Orinda.

7   Sandy Kimball, *Moraga's Pride: . . .*, 73.

8   Sandy Kimball, *Moraga's Pride: . . .*, 86-90.

9   Sandy Kimball, *Moraga's Pride: . . .*, 104.

10 Sandy Kimball, *Moraga's Pride: . . .*, 106. James Irvine had previously developed major land tracts in Orange County, creating the present-day city of Irvine. He also owned ranches in the San Joaquin and Imperial valleys. A man given to miserliness and with an autocratic nature—similar to Horace Carpentier—he was not an admired man.

11 Sandy Kimball, *Moraga's Pride: . . .*, 113-8. As part of the community planning effort, an aerial contour map was produced, which was the basis for the first master plan for the ranch.

12 Sandy Kimball, *Moraga's Pride: . . .*, 120. Donald Rheem was a son of the president of Standard Oil of California (now Chevron).

13 Sandy Kimball, *Moraga's Pride: . . .*, 121-4.

14 Sandy Kimball, *Moraga's Pride: . . .*, 126.

15 Sandy Kimball, *Moraga's Pride: . . .*, 124.

16 Sandy Kimball, *Moraga's Pride: . . .*, 125.

17 Sandy Kimball, *Moraga's Pride: . . .*, 126.

18 Sandy Kimball, *Moraga's Pride: . . .*, 126.

19 Richland Development Corporation subsequently sold the property to a new entity, Richfield Development Corporation. As of this writing (2024), the 123-home subdivision without golf course has been approved and is awaiting grading permits, according to Richfield. It's unclear just when Richfield intends to proceed.

20 Sandy Kimball, *Moraga's Pride: . . .*, 131-4.

21 Sandy Kimball, *Moraga's Pride: . . .*, 134.

22 The etymology of the city name Lafayette is described at https://en.wikipedia.org/wiki/Lafayette,_California, accessed Dec. 29, 2023.

23 Sandy Kimball, *Moraga's Pride: . . .*, 136.

24 The origin of the name Orinda is reported in https://en.wikipedia.org/wiki/Orinda,_California, accessed Dec. 29, 2023. (It's a bit more colorful than the Lafayette story.)

25 Also known as a "portmanteau." See https://en.wikipedia.org/wiki/Blend_word, accessed Dec. 29, 2023. The blend-word might have been coined by realtors in the Rancho area.

26 The Moraga Town Council approved the project, but that decision was reversed when several new council members were elected who opposed the project. Lafayette City Council was alleged to have colluded with the Moraga Council, which drew a lawsuit by the developer. The matter was settled by a court in Martinez.

27 Harre W. Demoro, *Sacramento Northern* (Wilton, Calif.: Signature Press, 1991). This book comprehensively describes the Sacramento Northern in detail from inception, through operations, and in its decline. Demoro provides detailed route maps, extensive photography of the rail system, and the stations and communities which it served. A companion document is Sam Sperry's brief document "Trains Through Moraga," prepared on behalf of the Moraga Historical Society as a teaching aid for school children (undated, unpublished).

28 Susan K. Skilton, *Images of America: Moraga* (Charleston, S.C.: Arcadia Publishing, 2016).

29 Sandy Kimball, *Moraga's Pride: . . .*, 162.

30 Sandy Kimball, *Moraga's Pride: . . .*, 172-3. The author was a commissioner on the Contra Costa Transportation Authority during the time of construction and opening of the Caldecott 4th Bore (2010-2013).

31 Sandy Kimball, *Moraga's Pride: . . .*, 165-71. These roadways, plus several others, are described in some detail.

32 Sandy Kimball, *Moraga's Pride: . . .*, 169-70. Kimball suggests that the Moraga segment of Bollinger Canyon Road would be more appropriately called Las Trampas Creek Road since it runs along the creek but has no connection to Bollinger Canyon Road on the east side of the Las Trampas Ridge. During the Cold War (1953-1962), a NIKE air defense system facility was built at the former site of the anti-aircraft installation.

33 State of California, Department of Public Works, Division of Highways, Dist. IV. CC-233-A, Exhibit "A", "Freeway in Contra Costa County Between the Alameda County Line and Route 75 (Drawing C "1229-2"), Dec. 1956.

34 Orinda-Moraga Homeowners Association and Utah Construction Company, "The Red Route is the Wrong Route: A Study by Engineers and Planners," 1956. This document was prepared and widely distributed. It explains that the so-called "Red Route" proposed by the California Highway Commission (CHC) was not the correct route for the Shepherd Canyon Freeway. Rather, a better route followed the SN Railway route down Pinehurst past present-day Canyon Village and entering Moraga along the railway route. But even this alternative route was strongly opposed by Moraga homeowners, who didn't want any freeway at all.

35 John Kaiser (ed.), "The Shepherd Canyon Highway 77 Controversy," *The Moraga Historical Society*, First Quarter 2024. This article summarizes the history and outcome of the controversy.

36 Sandy Kimball, 171-2. It must have been a shock for the California Highway Commission (now known as CalTrans) to realize that not everyone held so dear such ambitious plans for developing rural territory like the Moraga Valley. As for hopes for the region's traffic problems, recent history has amply demonstrated that BART has not been the panacea CalTrans had hoped for.

37 Sandy Kimball, *Moraga's Pride: . . .*, 172.

38 Sandy Kimball, *Moraga's Pride: . . .*, 142-3. The official name of the new town was the City of the Town of Moraga.

39 Sandy Kimball, *Moraga's Pride: . . .*, 146.

40 The steering committee for the 2002 General Plan update included two council members, two planning commissions, representatives from the Parks and Recreation Commission and Design Review Board, representatives of the major landowners, and small group of respected citizens. The committee made sweeping changes to the 1990 General Plan, and broke new ground on some major new policies governing growth in the downtown areas. But the most contentious issues involved large undeveloped land in Indian Valley and Bollinger Valley, owned by the Bruzzone family. (The author was one of the planning commissioners on the committee.)

41 Sandy Kimball, *Moraga's Pride: . . .*, 174-8. When the town limits were adjusted, the Moraga Adobe property became a part of Orinda, and exists that way to this day.

42 Sandy Kimball, *Moraga's Pride: . . .*, 180. The Moraga School District includes three elementary schools (Rheem, Los Perales, and Camino Pablo) plus Joaquin Moraga Intermediate. The Acalanes Union High School District includes four campuses (Campolindo, Miramonte, Acalanes, and Los Lomas (which serves a part of Walnut Creek)).

43 Sandy Kimball, *Moraga's Pride: . . .*, 198-200.

44 Revenue Enhancement Committee, "Final Report to the Moraga Town Council, November 18, 2009," 11. The report shows that Moraga's annual expenditures for police services on a per capita basis ($147) were considerably less than expenditures for Lafayette ($167) or Orinda ($195). (This committee is discussed in more detail in Chapter 4.)

45 Sandy Kimball, *Moraga's Pride: . . .*, 195-6.

46 Sandy Kimball, *Moraga's Pride: . . .*, 197.

47 Sandy Kimball, *Moraga's Pride: . . .*, 197. MOFD is responsible for 42 square miles of territory, including all of Moraga, Orinda, Canyon, and all unincorporated lands surrounding Moraga and Orinda. MOFD also has responsibilities for BART (within Lamorinda), three reservoirs, the Caldecott Tunnel, and St. Mary's College. Including all paid staff, elected officials, and all other volunteers, MOFD has eighty employees.

48 Sandy Kimball, *Moraga's Pride: . . .*, 201.

49 Access to the Moraga Commons was open to all, with some limitations of free use imposed by the town. However, one group of out-of-town folks somehow obtained the tacit approval of a town employee to construct a disc golf course on what is called the Back Forty portion of the Commons' land. These squatters became thoroughly established with the disc golf course, building permanent facilities and conducting regular tournaments. Around 2010, the squatters openly defied the town to make changes to the Commons' land that would encroach on their course. It was a remarkable display of chutzpah on their part. In the event, the town preferred not to cause an uproar over this encroachment . . . besides, it was known that there were Moraga citizens who also used the disc golf course on occasion.

50 This quotation was heard from the new town manager, who confided with the author when I had recently been elected the Town Council. The manager shared some of his conversations that he had had with angry Moraga citizens who could not understand how such a thing could have happened.

Chapter 4

1   Moraga's initial 1980 General Plan was revised in 1990, and again in 2002. The 2002 General Plan was a sweeping reformulation of the 1990 General Plan. Since then the plan has been amended six times (2010-2023). Each amendment has responded to changing conditions. The General Plan is scheduled for a significant rewrite in 2024.

As a Town of Moraga planning commissioner, the author was a member of the fifteen-member General Plan Steering Committee empaneled from 1999 through 2000. The committee was comprised of the mayor and one other Town Council member, two planning commissioners, a parks and recreation commissioner, a design review board member, a school board member, an MOFD commissioner, a representative of St. Mary's College, a chamber of commerce representative, a major landowner, and four citizens at large. The committee was supported by the town staff, led by the town manager. The team was supported by a cast of professional planners from eight planning consultancies, all from the Bay Area.

The 2002 General Plan is available for download on the town of Moraga web site (https://www.moraga.ca.us/).

See https://acrobat.adobe.com/id/urn:aaid:sc:us:a4766e76-df3a-4e14-9ced-0da7867161fa, accessed Jan. 5, 2024.

2   2002 General Plan, 2-1 and 2-2.

3   The values reported here are based on the author's eighteen years of experience as a planning commissioner (six years) and as a Town Council member (twelve years), including three one-year terms as mayor. One could quibble with any one of the stated values; disagreements with the author are expected. But the values as stated are personal observations, and the author is free to state them as he pleases.

4   The bronze plaque was a gift to Bill Snider, owner of Moraga Hardware & Lumber, by Dale Walwark, one-time member of the Moraga Town Council and a long-time resident of the town. According to Dale, he was given the plaque by his father-in-law, who acquired it in San Francsico in the 1930s.

Chapter 5

1   Readers are reminded that the formal name for Moraga is the "City of the Town of Moraga." All California's incorporated cities are "cities;" in Moraga's case, the name "Town of Moraga" reflects local insistence that the town is, in Moragans' eyes, a "town." To be called a "city" presumably denigrates Moraga's status as a small town. The Town of Danville, near Moraga, is also officially a city. Presumably Danville's small-town yearnings are reason for that town sharing Moraga's odd naming. This might be considered eccentric by some other Contra Costa County cities.

2   Several California cities operate with a "strong mayor" form of council. In these cases, a mayor is directly elected for that role to preside over the elected council members. The mayor supervises the manager, who is subordinate primarily to the mayor, but also to the council members. This form of government is usually seen in the larger cities; in Northern California, it has long been the form of government in San Francisco, Oakland, and San Jose. In Contra Costa County, it's the practice in Richmond, Martinez, and San Ramon, to name several.

3   A case of a council-manager relationship going sour developed in neighboring Lafayette. The story is told in a memoir by the Lafayette City Manager. Steven Falk, *California Story* (North Haven Conn.: Gas Can Press, 2023), 224-229). To paraphrase Falk's story:

In 2016 the California governor was forwarded legislation that decreed that any housing project that complied with local codes must be approved by the city/town in which the housing project was proposed; there could be no further local discretional review. This mandate caused an uproar in many California cities, especially in neighboring Lafayette. Residents who opposed the mandate were horrified that the State could impose its will on a local jurisdiction. The Lafayette City Council sided with the residents, despite the city manager's recommendation to abide by the State mandate. The council rejected the city manager's advice and later urged [him] "not to get ahead of the council on housing issues, with the inference that [he] should limit any land-use policy recommendations to options that would fly with residents." The city manager elected not to do that; instead, he continued to make his recommendation based on his best judgment and on prevailing practices elsewhere, leaving it to city council to reject or accept what he offered.

In 2017, based on the conviction that climate change was a factor in the wildfires that had recently ravaged Northern California, the State Legislature decreed that high-rise housing buildings must be accepted by local cities, regardless of their local zoning laws. The city manager agreed with the legislature, reasoning that properly built high-rise housing could be both affordable and reduce susceptibility to climate change. Public reaction to the prospect of high-rise housing adjacent to BART in downtown Lafayette was harsh. Nonetheless, the city manager endorsed the State mandate, to the chagrin of several Lafayette City Council members who couldn't understand why their city manager seemed insensitive to popular views. A compromise project was planned. But a petition launched to block the compromise project was approved by the voters. The city manager was dispirited; two years of work had gone down the drain. He confided in his memoir, "I could only conclude that I was out of sync with the majority of the people I'd served for so long."

Then in 2018, the State issued yet another mandate decreeing that high-rise housing must be built close by rail stations (meaning BART). The Lafayette City Council directed the city manager to challenge the mandate at a hearing in Sacramento. Neither the Lafayette mayor or vice-mayor could attend the hearing, leaving the city manager to represent and argue against the legislation, which he actually supported personally.

Upon returning to Lafayette, the city manager abruptly resigned.

It's perhaps unfair to consider the city manager's behavior to be insubordinate. Rather, it seems he resigned as a matter of conscience. He did not believe in what he was being instructed to do, so rather than simply accept the direction given him, he refused to go along. Some might have considered this insubordination. His decision seems to me an understandable one.

4   *General Plan* Policy FS1.2 - Contracting Services, 9-1.

5   *General Plan* Policy FS1 - Town Administration, Goal, 9-1.

6   *General Plan* Policy FS1.6 - Citizen Expertise, 9-1.

7   The League of California Cities is an organization whose members are all the cities and towns of California. The league conducts robust training programs for local officials, and cities are wise to send their elected and appointed officials to the courses wherever possible. The discussion in this chapter on "Dealing with Difficult People" was the subject of a half-day seminar at a training forum for city council members held in Monterey, California, in the fall of 2006. The seminar has helped the author dealing with those difficult people who have not been especially easy to handle.

The seminar was led by Dr. Rick Brinkman, who spoke for several hours on "How to bring out the best in people at their worst." His lecture was delivered (without any notes) in a delightful recitation of his bestselling book *Dealing with People You Can't Stand*, 3rd ed. (New York: McGraw-Hill, 2012), which he coauthored with his colleague Dr. Rick Kirschner.

8   Rick Brinkman and Rick Kirschner, *Dealing with People . . .*, xv.

9   Rick Brinkman and Rick Kirschner, *Dealing with People . . .*, 4-11. The characteristics of these problematic people are paraphrased from Brinkman and Kirschner's descriptions.

10   Rick Brinkman and Rick Kirschner, *Dealing with People . . .*, 39.

11   Rick Brinkman and Rick Kirschner, *Dealing with People . . .*, 63.

12   Rick Brinkman and Rick Kirschner, *Dealing with People . . .*, 72.

13   Rick Brinkman and Rick Kirschner, *Dealing with People . . .*, 78-80.

14   Tip O'Neill et al., *All Politics Is Local and Other Rules of the Game* (Holbrook, MA: Bob Adams, Inc, 1994), 174.

15   Rick Brinkman and Rick Kirschner, *Dealing with People . . .*, 84-0.

16   Rick Brinkman and Rick Kirschner, *Dealing with People . . .*, 98.

17   Rick Brinkman and Rick Kirschner, *Dealing with People . . .*, 127-35.

18   Rick Brinkman and Rick Kirschner, *Dealing with People . . .*, 108-16.

19   Rick Brinkman and Rick Kirschner, *Dealing with People . . .*, 137-50.

20   Rick Brinkman and Rick Kirschner, *Dealing with People . . .*, 118-24.

21   Rick Brinkman and Rick Kirschner, *Dealing with People . . .*, 151-60.

22   Rick Brinkman and Rick Kirschner, *Dealing with People . . .*, 161-71.

23   Rick Brinkman and Rick Kirschner, *Dealing with People . . .*, 173-81.

24   "Pygmalion effect" is a psychological phenomenon in which high expectations lead to improved performance in a given area and low expectations lead to worse. It's named for the Greek myth of Pygmalion, the sculptor who fell so much in love with the perfectly beautiful statue he created that the statue came to life. See Pygmalion Effect at https://en.wikipedia.org/wiki/Pygmalion_effect, accessed Jan. 9, 2024.

25   Rick Brinkman and Rick Kirschner, *Dealing with People . . .*, 251.

Chapter 6

1   Moraga 2002 General Plan, adopted June 4, 2002. Amended six times between 2010 through 2023. See General Plan page 1-12.

2   Moraga, like every city in California, is required to meet its State-mandated allocations for Regional Housing Needs Allocation (RHNA). A city's RHNA obligation is derived by allocating the statewide needs for new housing to all the counties; the counties then reallocate to their cities. Each city is then required to plan for the RHNA number of allocated housing units, and to encourage landowners and builders to build the units. Failure on a city's part to do the planning, or to obstruct development proposals, carries onerous penalties from the State, plus the prospects of legal action by housing advocacy groups. All the city can do is plan and encourage; it's up to the landowners and developers to build the housing.

3   The League of California Cities (also called Cal Cities) was founded in 1898, and has a membership that includes member cities and towns of California and professional organizations such as law firms specializing in administrative law. The league defends and expands local control through advocacy efforts in the State Legislature, at the ballot box, in the courts, and through strategic outreach that informs and educates the public, policymakers, and opinion leaders. Cal Cities also offers education and training programs designed to teach city officials about new developments in their field and exchange solutions to common challenges facing their cities. See https://www.calcities.org/about-us/, accessed Jan. 15, 2024.

4   Under federal legislation enacted in 2002 (Sarbanes-Oxley Act), auditing firms were prohibited from acting as management consultants for any of their audit clients. This prohibition adversely constrained the relationship between Moraga and their auditor. Advice could be offered only to the extent the advice pertained to the current audit.

5   Government Finance Officers Association letter to Moraga Town Manager, dated April 8, 2015, notifying of award qualification. GFOA is a professional organization that represents and serves federal, state/provincial,

and local finance officials in the U.S. and Canada. See https://community.gfoa.org/home, accessed Jan. 12, 2024.

6   Additional confirmation that things were going well in the Moraga finance realm came during the campaign for re-election in 2012. The *East Bay Times* conducted interviews of candidates for the council races of Contra Costa cities. Their chief interviewer (Daniel Borenstein) was a knowledgeable and tough individual, who said what he wanted and meant what he said. His principal interest was in public finance, and he was especially keen on the performance of elected officials in their handling of public financial matters. His political columns were widely respected. After the interview, Mr. Borenstein said to me that he considered Moraga to be one of the best-run cities from a financial operation standpoint. He admired what we had done, and he wanted me to know how he felt. I took great pleasure in reporting to my colleagues on the Town Council that we were held in such high regard.

7   Vera Kochan, "Moraga assigned AAA rating from S&P Global," *Lamorinda Weekly*, Dec. 20, 2023.

8   Town of Moraga. *Revenue Enhancement Committee, Final Report to the Moraga Town Council*, Nov. 2009.

9   The REC chairman was a senior citizen (Dick Olsen) who had been instrumental in formation of the town in 1974. He was on the committee that recommended formation of the Moraga Police Department, and he was part of the campaign to form MOFD. Other members included two council members (Dave Trotter and me), the town treasurer (Bob Kennedy, AFC Chair), Moraga Parks and Rec Department (Ravi Mallela), St. Mary's College (Zhan Li), Moraga School District (Kathy Ranstrom), Moraga Educational Foundation (Trish Bare), Moraga Chamber of Commerce (Larry Tessler), MOFD (Frank Sperling), and three citizens-at-large with broad experience in public and private finance (Fred Schroeder, Tracy Vesely, Tom Westhoff). The REC meet in noticed public meetings regularly from April-Dec. 2009.

10   Town of Moraga, *Revenue Enhancement Committee Final Report*, 1.

11   Town of Moraga, *Revenue Enhancement Committee Final Report*, Executive Summary, ii.

12   The method for selecting the focus group participants was to choose voters from the six voter precincts of the town as listed by the county recorder's voter rolls. The voter rolls were screened for active voters only (those voting in the past two general elections), and for residents of the town (excluding absentee voters). Eligible candidates for focus groups were randomly selected from each precinct list. Only a single voter per household/apartment was allowed in the group for the voter's precinct. The eligible candidates were contacted by telephone by a phone bank staffed by volunteers (mostly from the Moraga Kiwanis Club). Phone calls were made until ten candidates had committed to participating. Each one who committed was added to a focus group, regardless of their voting precinct. Because the voter precincts covered different sections of the town, geographic distribution of focus groups throughout the town was assured.

13   Each session was observed in the discussion room by two or three RECON committee members, which could include a maximum of two Town Council members (so as not to violate the Brown Act restrictions on non-noticed meetings by town officials). Observers were not allowed to participate in the discussions in any way; they could neither ask questions nor respond to questions that someone might pose. None of the sessions were recorded by either audio or video devices in the interest of participant confidentiality. The flip charts on which the recorders scribed during the meetings were the only record of the discussions.

14   The geographic distribution of the online survey was approximately even throughout the town; almost all responders were in households with two or more persons; most were long-time Moraga citizens (ten years or more); they were predominantly over age 40; half were employed, about 25 percent were retired. These demographics were similar to the focus group population.

15   Town of Moraga, *Revenue Enhancement Community Outreach to Neighborhoods (RECON). Committee Report to the Moraga Town Council and Public Forum*, July 28, 2010, 28.

16   Florence Laumanamea Brown, "Moraga Council Evaluates RECON, Looks to the Town's Financial Future," *Lamorinda Patch*, July 29, 2010.

17 "Moraga's Roads 'At Risk'," a presentation by RECON to the Moraga Town Council Nov. 3, 2011. The information that followed is from www.moraga.ca.us/documentcenter/view/528, accessed Jan. 16, 2024.

18 The Metropolitan Transportation Commission (MTC) is a government agency comprised of all 109 cities in the Bay Area of Northern California. MTC operates a robust department focused on pavement maintenance of Bay Area streets. One of the MTC tools is "StreetSaver," which inputs visual inspection (qualitative) data from road surveys, and crunches forecasts of pavement condition deterioration and costs projects for repair programs. The tool is used extensively by all Bay Area cities to plan their pavement maintenance programs. "StreetSaver" reports pavement conditions qualitatively and quantitatively in terms of a Pavement Condition Index (PCI): Excellent/Very Good (100-90), Good (89-70), Fair/At Risk (69-50), Poor (49-25), and Very Poor/Failed (24-0).

19 In a report dated June 2011 entitled "The Pothole Report: Can the Bay Area Have Better Roads?" MTC classified Moraga as one of the Bay Area cities with roads that were "At Risk." Moraga was ranked #93 out of 109 Bay Area cities that were classified. By comparison, Lafayette was ranked #45; Orinda, #105.

20 Sophie Braccini, "RECON on ROADS," *Lamorinda Weekly*, Sept. 28, 2011.

21 A certificate of participation (COP) is a type of financing where an investor purchases a share of the lease revenues of a program rather than a bond being secured by those revenues. Certificates of participation are secured by lease revenues, in Moraga's case, by new sales tax revenue. For information on COPs, see https://www.investopedia.com/terms/c/certificateofparticipation.asp, accessed Jan. 17, 2024.

22 The sales tax forecast was based on the town's history of taxable sales made within Moraga. Taxable sales would apply to items taxed by the State of California, but taxable items would be restricted to purchases made within the Town of Moraga. The 1 percent Moraga tax would be added to the California General Transaction and Use Tax (the State Sales Tax). The Moraga sales tax revenue, when added to existing revenues for road maintenance purposes (solid waste/garbage impact fees, gas tax, and sundry grant opportunities from the state and the county) would provide sufficient revenues to cover a long-term pavement maintenance program, assuming an intensive three-year program was completed.

23 In California, a tax for specific purpose is classified as a Special Tax, which requires a super majority for passage (two-thirds affirmative vote). However, a tax for undefined purposes is called a General Tax, which may not be directed to a sole purpose; rather, it must be available for general purposes. A General Tax requires only a simple majority of voters for approval (50 percent plus one, or more).

24 Town of Moraga Resolution No. 62-2012, July 25, 2012.

25 A public agency such as the Town of Moraga is prohibited from advocating for any measure put before the voters. No public funds may be used for any such advocacy. Rather, any citizen group may be formed to advocate for or against a ballot measure. Town employees are not allowed to be involved in any campaign work for any kind of advocacy unless they do so on their own time without any compensation involving public funds. Elected and appointed officials (all of whom are voters in the town) are at liberty to be involved.

26 *Town of Moraga, Voter Information Pamphlet containing Measure K—Town of Moraga*, Tues., Nov. 6, 2012.

27 Michael Metcalf and Dave Trotter were part of the committee. They were joined by Jill Keimach, the town manager, who attended meetings while on leave from her official duties. No committee members were affiliated with Town of Moraga government.

28 Sophie Braccini, "Town to Pursue the Purchase of New Property," *Lamorinda Weekly*, Dec. 9, 2009.

29 Sophie Braccini, "Town Staff to Leave Hacienda," *Lamorinda Weekly*, Aug. 15, 2012.

30 Town of Moraga, Staff Report to Town Council for Agenda Item 12.C, dated Jan. 13, 2016. This staff report requested that the council authorize filing a completion certificate for all works involved with the 335 Rheem project, including landscaping and all electronic systems, furniture, and equipment.

31 Sophie Braccini, "Moraga to Dedicate Veteran's Memorial," *Lamorinda Weekly*, Oct. 17, 2010.

32 It was never made clear how the School District drew this conclusion. The town's General Plan showed no such population growth; rather, population was expected to remain at the 17,000 level for a long time.

33 Staff report to Moraga Town Council and Moraga School District Board, "Request for Action," Agenda Item V.A, Jan. 20, 2015.

Chapter 7

1 Thomas Smith, "Rancho Laguna Park in Moraga; A Great Park Many Locals Haven't Heard Of," *Bay Area Telegraph*, July 25, 2023.

2 "Dusky-footed Wood Rat," in Wikipedia https://en.wikipedia.org/wiki/Dusky-footed_woodrat, accessed Feb. 12, 2024. This rodent is known to be a carrier of bubonic plague, although it's said there is minimal risk of present-day humans being seriously threatened by the plague brought by the Dusky-footed Wood Rat. See CBS New article at https://www.cbsnews.com/news/california-bubonic-plague-likely-catch/, accessed Feb. 12, 2024.

3 This was no frivolous petition. It had been pointed out by one dog enthusiast that, according to 2008 dog licensing records and voter data, about 7,000 Lamorinda voters could be dog owners. Of Lamorinda's 21,775 homes, 58 percent probably had a dog. Within this population, 67 percent of Moraga's 10,009 registered voters were likely dog owners. Even though this individual claimed not to be a political sort of person, he was clearly giving notice that popular voting was largely in favor of dog owners, which plainly meant the Town Council had better not do things that antagonized these voters. Can't get more political than that. "An open letter to Mayor Trotter and Members of the Moraga Town Council, from Bill Carmen," *Lamorinda Weekly*, April 15, 2009.

4 Sophie Braccini, quoting Council Member Howard Harpham in "Moraga Rescinds Dog Park Ordinance," *Lamorinda Weekly*, July 18, 2012. While nothing has been seen in the public record, there was a feeling at this time that the dog-parkers might resort to a "scorched earth" strategy if things didn't go their way. That wasn't a risk worth taking.

5 During these meetings, I discovered a new way to convince an agitated person that he should stop talking and take a seat: I intensely stared at an imaginary spot at the center of his forehead, above his eyes. After a few minutes, he would notice my stare. On one occasion he began to swat at his forehead, believing, I suppose, that there was an insect there. He did stop talking and took his seat. It was amusing . . . and quite effective.

6 Steve Angelides, "Moraga Road Bumps Land Council in Special Meeting," *Lamorinda Weekly*, September 5, 2007.

7 In the event, one council member proposed a compromise solution: remove two speed bumps but retain one at Camino Pablo School. His reasoning was that this would go toward appeasing those who wanted some traffic calming at the elementary school, but who wanted any speed bumps removed at the intermediate school. The proposal garnered council and public support, and that's what was agreed upon. (Nonetheless, the compromise never made much sense to me.)

8 Tip O'Neill, *Man of the House*, 338. As O'Neill would advise his younger colleagues in the House when he realized a mistake had been made: "Tell [people] the truth. . . . Come clean about it and do it quickly. Issue a statement saying that you were convinced by one set of arguments, but now that you've had a chance to hear the other side, you believe your earlier position was mistaken."

9 Steve Angeleides and Liz Borrowman, "Slow Down Lamorinda," *Lamorinda Weekly*, May 3, 2007, accessed Feb. 29, 2024.

10 Sophie Braccini, "A New Future for the Hacienda de las Flores," *Lamorinda Weekly*, May 6, 2015. In connection with comments by Council Member Dave Trotter calling the process to transform the Hacienda de las Flores one of the most interesting things he's worked on over his eight years on the Moraga Town Council.

11 Gould Evans, *Hacienda de las Flores: Conceptual Feasibility Study*, November 9, 2016.

12 In December 2016, the Town Council underwent annual reorganization. I had not run for re-election for a fourth term, which made December 14, 2016 my last Town Council meeting. By that time, matters concerning the Hacienda had slipped away from me.

13 Presently, Wedgewood continues to operate the Hacienda and provide wedding services to a robust nuptial market. While the town's financial problems are trending toward solution, aggravated neighbors have launched a campaign against the wedding business. Noise is the central issue. Both the town and Wedgewood are facing legal actions brought by various citizens who live close to the Hacienda. It's unclear how the legal squabbling will be resolved. If the town is forced to terminate the wedding business, then a public discussion will need to resume on what to do about the place. At that future time, perhaps the Town Council will appreciate what caused the phased approach to transform the Hacienda to fail. Maybe a plan can be worked out that is acceptable to most people and that works for the town financially.

14 Tip O'Neill, "Tip's Political Checklist," *All Politics Is Local and Other Rules of the Game* (Holbrook, Mass.: Bob Adams, Inc, 1994), 187.

15 Jaime Zepeda, "First Annual Moraga Triathlon," *Lamorinda Weekly*, May 3, 2007, accessed Feb. 28, 2024.

16 Chris Lavin, "Triathlon Lures 372 Athletes, One Bagpiper," *Lamorinda Weekly*, May 8, 2013, accessed Feb. 28, 2024.

17 The term "storm drain" refers to the pipes, culverts, and ditches that convey water. This drainage is separate from "sanitary drains" which convey sewage. The sanitary sewers are owned and operated by a separate agency, not the Town of Moraga. The storm drain system is under the town's purview.

18 Schaaf & Wheeler Consulting Civil Engineers, Executive Summary, "Moraga Storm Drain Master Plan," July 2015.

19 Sophie Braccini, "State of Emergency Declared in Moraga," *Lamorinda Weekly*, March 23, 2016. See also "San Bruno pipeline explosion," Wikipedia, at https://en.wikipedia.org/wiki/San_Bruno_pipeline_explosion, accessed Jan. 31, 2024.

20 Sophie Braccini, "Corroded Culvert is to Blame for Sinkhole," *Lamorinda Weekly*, May 4, 2016.

21 The "protest ballot" process in California provides that an agency that imposes a property-related fee for services must allow those households subject to the fee to register their protest in a secret election. If 50 percent plus one vote protests the fee, the fee cannot be enacted. This election requirement is imposed by Section 6(c) of Article XIIID, added to the State of California Constitution in 1996 by Prop 218. Certain services such as water and sewer are exempt from this requirement. However, the language of Prop 218 did not provide a clear definition of "sewer," so in 2002, an appellate court ruled that storm drainage was not exempt. Then the State Legislature enacted SB231, which stated that storm drainage was to be considered sewer and therefore exempt from the ballot requirement. This put the legislature in conflict with the court on the matter of interpreting the State Constitution. Thus, the Town of Moraga was put in the position of having to decide whether to follow the direction of the court, or of the legislature. On the advice of a competent municipal finance advisor, the town chose not to follow SB231, since to do so, would invite a legal challenge from taxpayer advocacy organizations (namely, Howard Jarvis Taxpayer Association). Given that the legal expense to the town of defending itself against a challenge would far exceed the $140,000 cost of an election, the town chose to follow the court ruling and proceed with a protest ballot. See finance advisor's explanation of this situation: Sam Sperry, "SB 231 Question," Letter to The Editor, *Lamorinda Weekly*, April 4, 2018.

22 Sophie Braccini, "Pros and cons of the stormwater fee," *Lamorinda Weekly*, April 4, 2018. The SOS representatives included myself (no longer on the Town Council), John Hafner (chair of the SOS committee), and Dale Walwark. The cited article reported the responses to the questions posed by the reporter. SmartMoraga (SM) was represented by Brent Meyers and Scott Bowhay. The SM people styled themselves as overseers of the town's management. By the name they chose for their organization, they were advertising themselves as all-knowing; their word was to be trusted, not the town's. Many people did not appreciate their approach, yet SM did succeed in scuttling the storm drain fee.

23 Town of Moraga Staff report to Town Council dated May 23, 2018. See https://www.moraga.ca.us/DocumentCenter/View/3686/Council-05-23-18-Stormwater-Ballot-Certification-PDF, accessed March 1, 2024.

24 Nick Marnell, "A town on the brink," *Lamorinda Weekly*, Dec. 13, 2017. This article contains half-truths and misleading information. It was not at all helpful in providing Moraga readers a fair picture of what had been happening and what was coming down the road. This reporter reminded me of what Tip O'Neill had said about Sam Donaldson, a correspondent for ABC News. Donaldson had a reputation for being tough on everyone he interviewed. O'Neill wrote in his memoir, "My beef is not with Sam Donaldson, but with the young reporters around the country who try to emulate Sam's aggressive posture without really knowing the issues. These guys are just showing off, and they don't add anything to the public's understanding of the news." (Tip O'Neill, *Man of the House*, 272.)

25 "Storm Drain Fee," Bobbie Preston, Letter to the Editor, *Lamorinda Weekly*, April 4, 2018, accessed Feb. 15, 2024.

26 The *Marketplace Facilitator Act* was added by Assembly Bill (AB) 147 and amended by State Bill 92. The amended act provided that beginning October 1, 2019, a marketplace facilitator is generally responsible for collecting, reporting, and paying the tax on retail sales made through their marketplace for delivery to California customers. Amazon is deemed to be a marketplace facilitator for third-party sales through Amazon's global marketplace. Other telemarketers are similarly obliged. See "Tax Guide for Marketplace Facilitator Act," California Department of Tax and Fee Administration, www.catfa.ca.gov, accessed Jan. 30, 2024.

Chapter 8

1 Kare Anderson, "Who Packs Your Parachute?" *Forbes*, Nov. 18, 2015. This article is about Charles Plumb, a U.S. Navy jet fighter pilot who flew missions over Vietnam from the *USS Kitty Hawk*. Plumb was shot down and parachuted into North Vietnam, where he was held as a prisoner of war. Years later in America, Plumb was approached by a man who recognized him. He told Plumb that he had packed Plumb's parachute aboard the *Kitty Hawk*. Plumb didn't know the man, but he sure appreciated that the man had packed his parachute. The encounter got Plumb, now a motivational speaker by profession, to thinking that it's important to recognize people, even if you don't know anything about them, because you never know: They might be the one who packs your parachute.

2 Case in point was the election for open Town Council seats in 2018. Two seats were being contested. The SmartMoraga folks, fresh off their victory in defeating the Storm Drain Fee, were challenged by several citizens (myself included) to run for office. None of them would consider it. While they had the time to prepare cases against anything the town was trying to do, they didn't have the time to help out in constructive ways. In my view, they weren't worth being taken seriously.

3 Tip O'Neill, *All Politics Is Local and Other Rules of the Game* (Holbrook, Mass., Bob Adams, Inc, 1994), 95-6.

4 Tip O'Neill, *All Politics Is Local. . . .*, 95.

5 Private conversation with Gayle Uilkema, Contra Costa Board of Supervisors, in 2005, soon after I was first elected to the Moraga Town Council.

6 Tip O'Neill, *Man of the House,* 238.

7 Tip O'Neill, *All Politics Is Local. . . .*, 187-8.

8 Tip O'Neill, *All Politics Is Local. . . .*, 187-8.

Bibliography

"Blend Word." In *Wikipedia*, December 26, 2023. https://en.wikipedia.org/w/index.php?title=Blend_word&oldid=1191953722.

Brinkman, Rick, and Rick Kirschner. *Dealing with People You Can't Stand: How to Bring Out the Best in People at Their Worst*. Rev. and Expanded 3rd ed. New York: McGraw-Hill, 2012.

Chen, James. "Certificate of Participation (COP)," April 24, 2022. https://www.investopedia.com/terms/c/certificateof participation.

Demoro, Harre W. *Sacramento Northern*. Second printing, with minor corrections, February 2010. Wilton and Berkeley, California: Signature Press, 2010.

Diamond, Jared M. *Collapse: How Societies Choose to Fail or Succeed*. New York, New York: Penguin Books, 2011. http://www.mackin.com/BookPics/Book.aspx?isbn=9780143117001.

Evans, Gould. "Hacienda de Las Flores: Conceptual Feasibility Study." Town of Moraga, November 9, 2016.

ExxonMobil Corporation. "PNG Gas Project." ExxonMobil. Accessed December 15, 2023. https://www.pnglng.com/about.

Falk, Steven. *California Story*. North Haven, Connecticut: Gas Can Press, 2023.

Kimball, Sandy. *Moraga's Pride: Rancho Laguna de Los Palos Colorados*. 2nd ed. rev. and Expanded. Moraga, CA (P.O. Box 103, Moraga 94556): Moraga Historical Society, 2002. http://catdir.loc.gov/catdir/toc/fy0603/2001098755.html.

"Lafayette, California." In *Wikipedia*, November 4, 2023. https://en.wikipedia.org/w/index.php?title=Lafayette,_California&oldid=1183504928.

Lamorinda Weekly. *Lamorinda Weekly*, n.d. https://lamorindaweekly.com/html2/archive.html.

O'Neill, Tip, and Gary Hymel. *All Politics Is Local, and Other Rules of the Game*. Holbrook, Mass.: B. Adams, 1995.

O'Neill, Tip, and William Novak. *Man of the House: The Life and Political Memoirs of Speaker Tip O'Neill*. St. Martin's Press, Mass Market Edition. New York, New York: Random House, 1988.

"Orinda, California." In *Wikipedia*, November 27, 2023. https://en.wikipedia.org/w/index .php?title=Orinda,_California&oldid=1187121114.

Popik, Barry. "The Big Apple: 'All Politics Is Local.'" Accessed June 27, 2023. https://www .barrypopik.com/index.php/new_york_city/entry/all_politics_is_local/.

Schaaf & Wheeler. "Moraga Storm Drain Master Plan." Town of Moraga, July 2015.

Smith, Thomas. "Rancho Laguna Park in Moraga: A Great Park Many Locals Haven't Heard Of." *Bay Area Telegraph*, July 25, 2023.

Skilton, Susan K. *Images of America: Moraga*. Charleston, SC: Arcadia Publishing, 2016.

"Tengiz Field." In *Wikipedia*, August 15, 2023. https://en.wikipedia.org/w/index .php?title=Tengiz_Field&oldid=1170484216.

Town of Moraga. "Revenue Enhancement Committee Final Report to the Moraga Town Council." Unpublished, November 2009. Town of Moraga archive.

———. "Town of Moraga 2002 General Plan with Amendments." Town of Moraga, June 4, 2002.

———. "Town of Moraga Document Center," n.d. https://www.moraga.ca.us /documentcenter/.

"Wikipedia Online Encyclopedia," n.d. https://en.wikipedia.org/wiki/.

Acknowledgments

NO ONE IN PARTICULAR inspired me to write this book. I alone am responsible for that. It had occurred to me, well into my golden years, that I ought to commit to paper some recollections of things past, and assess whether I had been leading a useful life. Like many of my friends in the Town of Moraga, where I have lived with my family for nearly 40 years, upon retirement from professional life to community service, I dedicated myself to volunteering for an appointed position in the town. This led to my election to the Town Council. During what followed to be 18 years of public service, I was able to achieve a lot of things that probably helped the town. Of course, I made a lot of mistakes. Overall, the effort was worth my while, and I suspect that a number of Moragans would agree that my efforts benefited many.

Some people certainly helped me along the way. Professor Hank Parker, a mentor at Stanford University, inspired me to think about the succession of careers that people like me can take. "Have the courage to branch out," advised Hank. And that's what I did. My service to Moraga was my third career, and entirely different from the first two.

Upon joining the Moraga Town Council, I received an excellent suggestion from another marvelous mentor, Gayle Uilkema, Contra Costa County Supervisor. "Show up!" That was simple. I didn't realize at the time how important her words would be in the coming years. I did show up faithfully and people did notice. They rewarded me for it, and no doubt for other reasons, with re-election two more times.

The "council-manager" form of government practiced by Moraga depends on good-faith relationships between the town manager and the Town Council. As mayor, I had the pleasure of working closely with two excellent professionals who were also delightful people. Mike Segrest was the breath of fresh air that Moraga needed to begin the long move into modernity. Jill Keimach was the charming and sharp-minded manager who brought home many of the enduring good things in the town's government. Both of these exceptional people taught me a lot about how to get things done—and steered me clear of committing blunders. Together with an extraordinary town attorney, Michelle Kenyon, I always knew I had dependable and honest allies with me and sound counsel on which I could rely. These three public servants set the bar high for others to clear.

Colleagues on the Town Council were a varied lot. Most notable and appreciated were Howard Harpham and Dave Trotter. Howard, an attorney by profession, had a dry sense of humor and keen insight that brought needed clarity to many complex issues. Dave's direct and forceful approach, while at times trying, never rose to where I wouldn't listen to his views. Also an attorney by profession, his thinking was clear. His legal background, expertise in planning and land use, and knowledge of municipal law helped enormously to resolve some tough questions during our years on the Town Council. We achieved a lot of good things for the town. In addition, Dave reviewed the manuscript for this book thoroughly and offered myriad excellent suggestions for improvement.

Dick Olsen, one of the original incorporators of the town, was a wonderful colleague in the realm of revenue enhancement and in the campaign to fix Moraga's roads. His sharp mind and crisp insights help push over the line one of the most important voter propositions since town incorporation. Sam Sperry, a retired municipal finance attorney, was of invaluable assistance in fashioning the financing scheme that enabled the town to fund the massive road repair program that the voters approved. Both of these gentlemen have broad knowledge of the town's storied past, and in detail. And over the years, both have helped me understand Moraga much better than I ever could have on my own.

Renata Sos, my longtime neighbor and the first political adviser to help me out on my maiden campaign for Town Council, also reviewed the manuscript and graciously offered her comments. As a current Town Council member and former mayor, she appreciates the sensitivity of public relationships. She is an especially insightful attorney who understands how government works, and how to make things happen.

My publisher, Linda Roghaar, once again, has mobilized her publishing services team to the publication of this book, the fifth book I have asked her to do. Jean Stone as copyeditor, has transformed my at-times arduous engineering-like prose into copy that's readable. Book design, inside and out, has been done by Doug Lufkin. His exquisite taste in how a book should look and feel contributes much to the success of a good publication. Janet Blowney has done all the proofreading, ensuring that everything is correct, makes sense, and ties together. Very little slips by her keen eye.

Lastly, a work of thanks to my faithful wife, Sharon. She put up with me spending countless days and nights working on town business while she was doing the lioness's share of running the household and raising the children. Now that I've found a niche in writing about the past, she continues to be remarkably tolerant. I much appreciate her indulgence and love her for it.

About the Author

MICHAEL FRENCH METCALF is a native New Englander. He was raised in Concord, Massachusetts where he attended Middlesex School, preparing for undergraduate education at the University of Pennsylvania. Earning a degree in civil engineering, he joined the U.S. Navy as an officer in the Civil Engineer Corps. After two tours with the Navy Seabees in Vietnam, and several years as an Officer in Charge of Construction in Thailand, he was discharged from the Navy. He received masters and PhD degrees in civil engineering from Stanford University. After a long career in the petroleum industry as a engineering and construction project manager, he entered public service in the Town of Moraga, his home for many years. After 18 years in appointed and elected positions with the town, he retired to a life of writing. This book is his fifth publication; the first and third were family histories: *Inklings: John Wilkins Carter and the Carter's Ink Company*, and *Michael Metcalf(e), the Dornix Weaver, and Some Dedham Descendants*.

Milton Keynes UK
Ingram Content Group UK Ltd.
UKHW050751141024
449707UK00016B/165